© 2024 Antonio Stuckey

Cover by Adriana Elizabeth

All rights Reserved under International and Pan-American Copyright Conventions. No Part of this book may be reproduced in any form or by any electronic means, including information storage and retrieval systems, without permission in writing from the publisher, except by a reviewer who may quote brief passages in a review.

"The Fell Types are digitally reproduced by Igino Marini. www.iginomarini.com"

ISBN: 979-8-3304-3316-2

Sober and civil

Being a true narrative of one Sarah Towne Cloyse, formerly Bridges

Written by Antonio Stuckey

Cover Design by Adriana Elizabeth

To my Mom and Nana

To my best friends, Adriana and Indie, for listening

To the Rebecca Nurse Homestead Crew

To the Massachusetts Witch Hunt Justice Project

And to Sarah Cloyse, for fighting and surviving so I could tell your story.

Table of Contents

Chapter 1

7

Chapter 2

21

Chapter 3

36

Chapter 4

45

Chapter 5

57

Chapter 6

75

Chapter 7

95

Chapter 8

112

Chapter 9

129

Chapter 10

146

Chapter 11

166

Authors Note and Acknowledgments   192

Endnotes   195

Part 1:
1620-1691

Chapter 1
Before Sarah

The Townes of Yarmouth

In 1620, a young couple stood in the old medieval Church; their marriage read out as a legal deal rather than a declaration of love. They signed the document sealing their union as William and Joanna Towne; soon, they would give birth to a healthy baby girl named Rebecca. Growing up in the crowded old medieval city made life difficult, the plague, war, and religion. This was hardly a life for a multiplying family; after Rebecca, they had John, February 1623; Susan, October 1625; Edmund, June 1628; Jacob, March 1632; Mary, August 1634. Sadly, young Susan would pass before she would grow into adulthood, at the young age of five years old—a sad but normal part of day-to-day life in the 17th Century.

During this time, the Townes were like many others in Yarmouth, were Puritans, a sect of the Protestant religion that had more radical views than the Church of England. John Calvin influenced many

Puritan's hope to purify the Church of England and Christianity from any Catholic images and views. However, they did allow infant baptism and the Lord's supper (communion) into their sacraments. This was against the teachings of the Church of England, had Henry VIII not wanted a divorce from Katharine of Aragon to marry Anne Boleyn. Succeeded by his Protestant son Edward VI, then the attempted Catholic restoration during Mary I. The reign of Elizabeth I saw the development of the Protestant faith and more sects of the religion. After the death of Elizabeth I and the ascension of the Scottish King James VI to the English Throne, the crackdown against Puritans began.

      Laws were established, Puritans were being persecuted, and the monarchy religion was still unstable. James I was disliked by the Puritans, and his son Charles I was despised by them. Having married a Catholic was something that many Puritans feared as the downfall of the Protestant religion. The group that feared this were called Separatists, who wanted to see complete removal of Catholic influence from the Church of England. Some separatists fearing the downfall of Protestantism left England around 14 years before creating their settlement to practice religion freely. This was one of the many reasons the Townes and other Puritan families left England to create their own new "pure" society, their "City on the Hill."

    William and Joanna Towne were officially seen as Separatists in 1633 when they didn't attend communion in the Church. They soon began planning to leave England, which would happen in the next two years. They wanted to join the other Puritans like themselves in the City on the Hill; however, the process to leave England was complex, needing permission from the Privy Council to leave. In his book *A Salem Witch,* author Dan Gagnon writes, "These restrictions might be a reason for lack of contemporary documentation on when the Townes left for New England: only those names of people who left legally were officially recorded."

    The voyage would have been challenging, with small ships with at least a hundred people. Depending on the time of year, it could take weeks to months, depending on the weather and whether the winds are favorable. When the Townes left

England, it was just William, Joanna, and their children: Rebecca, Edmund, Jacob, and barely a year-old daughter, Mary. Their other son Jacob became an apprentice in Yarmouth, chose to stay behind. They could've been caught and detained, but the small ship slipped its moorings and sailed from the harbor with a gust of wind. Out onto the blue Atlantic Ocean, a new life and world for the Townes and other families to begin anew.

Early Salem

When the Townes arrived nine years after the original settlement in 1626, they lived on a ten-acre plot in a section of Salem known as "Northfields." Arriving in Salem at some point in 1635, the Townes built a small temporary shelter similar to the local Indigenous tribes' wigwams. After some time, William Towne and other men built more studier structures, likely a two-room home "half house." The roof is thatched or finished with wooden shingles, and the exterior finished with clapboards and clay walls on the interior, unlike their original home in England, which was likely a stone shelter in Great Yarmouth.

Sarah Towne, was born in this two-room home on an unrecorded date between 1641 and 1642. Her mother was around forty-seven, and her father was forty-three; she would be the last child of William and Joanna. She may have been the baby of the Towne family, but as time shows, she grows into a strong and formidable woman. This trait is seen in many of the Towne women in 17th-century records. Exhausted from the labor, Joanna held her baby, swaddled in a linen cloth, her little body cleaned. Named Sarah, after the wife of Abraham in the Old Testament, she was seen as the Mother of the Jewish people. The name meant "princess" in Hebrew, a name fit for the family's youngest child.

While the names Rebecca, Mary, and Sarah were common among their fellow Puritan women, remarkably, they fit the characters of the women they are named after. In the book of Genesis, Rebecca was told, "*And they blessed Rebekah, and said unto her, Thou art our sister, be thou the mother of thousands of millions, and let thy seed possess the gate of those which hate them.*" She would go on to produce eight healthy children. Mary, named after the

Mother of Christ, was seen as a saint. Sarah, much like her counterpart in the Bible, is loving, steadfast, and authoritative.

    Sarah and the younger Towne children didn't have time to play; as they grew, they were expected to help with the chores around the farm. Every day, there was work to be done, and the only day where they could "rest" was Sunday, when they spent most of their day at Sunday service at the Meeting House in Salem Town. Built near the intersection of (present-day) Essex Street and Washington Street, the Meeting House the Townes attended was built around the time they arrived in 1635. Services were long, led by the Reverend Edward Norris, who began preaching in the early Winter of 1640. Governor John Winthrop described Norris as "grave and judicious," a man of talent, good judgment, and tolerance.

    Norris and most Puritan ministers preached sermons, which are now seen as "fire and brimstone" preachings. Sermons preaching against frivolous amusement, believing that all men were born sinners since Adam's fall. Believing that they were predestined for hell unless they were one of the "elect" and meant to be saved. Religion was a large part of everyday life for families at this time, with most homes only having books, such as the Bible, a Psalm book, and an almanac. When something went wrong, they prayed; when something wonderful happened, they prayed. All in the hope that they could be one of God's elect, saving their souls from eternal damnation in hell.

Life in the Town

The household shrunk by one in 1644; the eldest of the Towne children, Rebecca, married Francis Nurse. A tray maker who was once brought to court for breaking into a home was around Rebecca's age of 23. Within a year, she would give birth to the first of what would be eight children: John (1645), Rebecca (1647), Samuel (1649), Sarah (c. 1651), Mary (1659), Francis Jr (1661), Elizabeth (1663), and Benjamin (1666). She and her new husband would relocate to the area near present-day Bridge Street in Salem; they lived here until about 1664 and, in 1678, moved further inland to Salem Village.

On June 13th, 1648, Joanna became a Covenant Member of the Salem Town Church, and less than a month later, on July

3rd, 1648, the youngest two Towne children, Sarah and Joseph, were baptized.

Amazingly, many of Joanna's children would be entered into full Church Membership throughout the area. Becoming a covenant member of the church meant they were among the elect and God's chosen; their souls saved from damnation. Rebecca would find membership and a place among Christ's chosen at the Salem Town Church in 1672, Mary in Topsfield c. 1670s, and Sarah at Salem Village Church in 1689. Joanna relied upon Rebecca, the eldest daughter, to assist with household chores and the children. Being the eldest daughter, she had to assist in the chores in the house and the garden, just as the male Towne children had to help their father with the chores in the fields. Skills the children needed to know when the time came for them to grow up and marry and raise their own families. However, upon Rebecca's marriage, the next eldest daughter, Mary Towne, around sixteen, became her mother's biggest helper. Early on, colonists would have to order their materials if they couldn't make their clothing. However, as the population grew, more experienced weavers and tailors came to Salem, and colonists would weave their cloth to bring to tailors to make up into clothing.

    Flax was commonly used, made into linen, for making coifs, neckerchiefs, shifts, and clothing. Alongside linen was wool, which, depending on the quality, could be cheap or expensive. Shearing the sheep, cleaning it, carding it, then spinning it into yarn could take about a day. Once the yarn was spun, it could be woven into woolen cloth; there were different types of wool depending on the weave and finish. Most of the time, linen and wool were mixed into "*linsey-woolsey*" and used for garments—bodices and petticoats.

    Color was prevalent in Puritan society, not the typical blacks and grays that modern media would suggest. Natural dyes, including yellows, blues, greens, and reds, were plentiful. Mixing colors to create light purples was common, too. However, dress was regulated by Sumptuary Laws, which restricted clothing for the wearer depending on their social status.

"The Court, taking into consideration the great, superfluous, & unnecessary expenses

occasioned by reason of some new & immodest fashions, as also the ordinary wearing of silver, gold, & silk laces, 'girdles, hatbands, &c, hath therefore ordered that no person, either man or woman, shall hereafter make or buy any apparel, either woolen, silk, or linen, with any lace on it, silver, gold, silk, or thread, under the penalty of forfeiture of such clothes, &c."

People were often fined for breaking the sumptuary laws; in 1653, Frances Hutchins, who was accused of Witchcraft in 1692, was brought to court in Ipswich for wearing a silk hood. The Towne family and their peers would've dressed simply, men in a linen shirt, weskit (waistcoat), breeches, and a frock coat and women in a linen shift, boned bodice (later separate stays were more popular by the end of the 17th Century) or gown, a few petticoats, and a coif to cover the hair. Both genders wore stockings and shoes, which were generally knitted and darned regularly.
Common folk generally had one set of nice clothing for Church on Sundays and possibly an extra bodice and petticoat or waistcoat. However, the wardrobe selection

was small, leading to certain aspects of one's clothing being an easily identifiable trait. Many people accused of Witchcraft during the 1692 outbreak were identified by their clothing since it was so recognizable. However, Salem isn't the first case in which someone accused was recognized by their clothing; previous examples of accusations show clothing being used as an identifying trait.

~~~

Things would change for the Towne Family beginning in the 1650s. Edmund Towne was next to be wed in 1652 when he married Mary Browning. William Towne sold his ten acres of land in Salem, relocating the family to a larger plot in Topsfield. The new Towne Farm was on forty acres of land in Topsfield, near the Ipswich River, at the present-day intersection of South Main Street and Salem Street. Edmund and his wife Mary would start their family in a home that was built nearby; there they would raise their nine surviving children: Mary (c. 1653), Thomas (c. 1655), Sarah (1655), William (1658),

Joseph (1661), Abigail (1664), Rebecca (1668), Elizabeth (1669), Samuel (1672). They also had three children who would die young, either at birth or before the age of ten.

    Sarah's elder sister Mary was next, marrying Issac Esty in 1655; she, too, would build her family close to her parents' farm. Mary would go on to have nine children: Isaac Jr (c. 1656), Joseph (1659), Sarah (1660), John (1663), Hannah (c. 1667), Benjamin (1669), Samuel (1672), Jacob (1675), and Joshua (1678). Mary and her Towne siblings, who stayed in Topsfield, would grow to become respected community members—becoming church members, tithingmen, constables, and jurors to help the community and build a good and respectable reputation. Even in 1692, among most of the community, the accusations against Sarah and her sisters shocked many in the Town.

    Jacob Towne would marry in 1657 to Katherine Symonds and would go on to have six children together and live in Salem Town until Joanna died in 1683. Sarah's turn for the marriage market came in early 1660. Sarah married Edmund Bridges Jr, to

Edmund Bridges Sr, born October 4th, 1637, in Massachusetts. The early origins of the Bridges family are unclear; we know that Edmund Sr came to Massachusetts in 1635 at twenty-three aboard the ship "*James.*" He would settle in Lynn and work as a Blacksmith after his arrival.

From here, his story gets muddled in the historical record; some historians state that Edmund Sr. first married a woman named either Alice or Elizabeth. Both Father and Son would work as blacksmiths and attorneys, which, in the later run, would muddle the record between the two when it would come to later court cases in later years. Sarah would wed Edmund in a simple ceremony before a Magistrate; forgoing an engagement, they would've had a brief courting phase. They would've likely married in the Topsfield Meeting House, signing a document that sealed their union as husband and wife.

The couple settled on the Topsfield-Salem Village border; their property was about eight acres southeast of Rhea's Hill, near present-day John Lane in Topsfield. The couple's farm and Edmund's blacksmith shop provided well for the family and had a small but decent plot of land on the common, for which Edmund paid 15 shillings. One can surmise Sarah's hope for a comfortable future, her husband doing well in his trade and on the farm. Within a few months of marriage, Sarah learned she was pregnant and would give birth to a son, Edmund Bridges III, on October 4th, 1660.

     Over the next few years, Sarah would give birth to three children: on January 2nd, 1665, a son named Benjamin; on April 14th, 1667, a daughter named Mary; and on June 9th, 1669, a daughter named Hannah. By the end of the decade, Sarah and Edmund had two more children, Caleb and Alice, all of whom had survived their early years. The success of the Towne family in producing healthy children is astonishing; Rebecca, Mary, and Sarah would all have around eight or nine children, all of whom would make it to adulthood. Even their brothers would have success, losing only around three children out of the twelve in the case of Edmund Towne. A young mother at 18 years old, newly married, and grateful to her God for the future, she likely never saw what would come in the next thirty-two years.

Chapter 2
Troubled Times in Topsfield

The first few years of the Bridges' marriage went well; Edmund continued his work on the farm with Sarah's assistance and his work as a blacksmith and attorney. Edmund had no legal training, but his father's work helped him gain experience. His work also brought him close to the Putnam family of nearby Salem Village. Edmund worked closely with John and Nathaniel Putnam, in many court cases.

Sarah was busy with her work at home, using the skills taught to her by her mother. Cooking in the hearth, spinning threads, and weaving cloth, working in the gardens that sat not too far outside. The Bridges' home, built on a small eight-acre plot, was likely similar to the homes where Sarah had grown up: two rooms, a ground floor, and a floor above, accessible by ladder or stairs to reach the top. Small windows let light in, most likely oiled paper instead of glass diluted it, as glass would've been expensive for the working-class Bridges family.

    Work began for Sarah and Edmund around 4:30-5 am. They would work from sun up to sun down and return to bed exhausted around 8 pm. Depending on the day, Edmund would work for the local courts, settling disputes between neighbors, with Sarah occasionally giving depositions as well. The first case in which Sarah's name appears to give a deposition is a 1664 case regarding one of her "sisters." John Millington was sentenced to be whipped in March 1664, the reason being having committed a "great misdemeanor" against an unnamed woman.

    In her book "*Currents of Malice*", Persis McMillen discusses the case and theorizes that because Sarah referred to the woman as "her sister," she is referring to Mary Esty. However, it also points out that Mary's age at the time, around thirty-five, is likely not her; other possibilities included Faith Black, Edmund's sister, who was married to Daniel Black in a rather unhappy marriage. Meeting at the Ipswich Court, the unnamed woman deposed, and a few months prior, in January, her brother Edmund

Bridges (Jr) asked her to accompany him to Salem.

The unknown woman declined going with them, so Edmund and Sarah left without her. Then, John Millington came to the house and offered "uncleanliness" to her. She responded, "*She would not yield to him for all of Topsfield,*" Millington would later testify that he prayed for forgiveness from the unknown woman. Sarah testified that "her sister" sent Millington to the house for some meal (likely for bread making). But no further deposition was given, and the case ended with the woman's identity unknown.

Unfortunately, the identity remains unknown, the reason for the blocking out remaining an almost 350-year-old mystery. McMillen also points out that Sarah and Edmund deposed against Millington, who John Gould bailed out.

Issues with John Gould

John Gould was born in England c. 1635 to Zaccheus and Phebobe Gould; the family would come to Massachusetts a few years after the Townes in 1638. The Goulds likely started in Weymouth, and eventually, over the years, they would settle in Topsfield by the end of the 1650s. The Goulds would become prominent landowners in Topsfield, building their roots in the community. In the same 1661 record showing the division of the Common Land, the most considerable portion was purchased by John and his Father Zaccheus at 4 pounds, 3 shillings, and 3 pence.

    Edmund went into business with John Gould in 1668. Rowley Village (Boxford) opened an ironworks due to the closing of the one in Saugus in 1668. The land it had been built on had been left to John by his Father and was built due to the demand for iron. Items such as iron had to be imported from England, which could take months to arrive in the colonies. So, such steps were necessary for colonists to make their lives easier. It's suggested that Edmund wasn't fully involved in the production of iron, but rather, he got involved because of his trade as a blacksmith.

    However, the Iron Works venture caused problems for the Bridges and Gould men; in November 1670, John Gould brought Edmund Bridges to court in Salem Town. Before they started the Iron Works, Edmund had somehow gotten in debt with

Gould. So, as a result, John sued Edmund for "*Not fulfilling a bargain in setting his hand to a deed of sale of land.*" The court demanded that Edmund either pay 150 pounds to John or sign over the deed of his land to John Gould. Unfortunately, Edmund lost his home, barn, and land on December 9th, 1670.

    In the same document, Phillip Welch testified that the winter prior in 1669, he went with John Gould to the home of Isaac Esty, Edmund's brother-in-law. Jacob Towne was also in the home, and Welch stated, "*Edmund Bridges came in, who is conversing with Jacob Towne and Issac Esty about getting clapboards* (siding) *for his house. Not knowing where to get them, desired Ens. John Gould to let him get them upon this division.*" The record further states, "*Deponent asked if this division was his or Ens. Gould's, to which Bridges replied he had nothing to do with it,*" The apparent tension between Edmund and his brother-in-law's Jacob and Isaac piques interest.

    With the interest of Sarah's parents, William and Joanna, her siblings and sister-in-law, Joseph and Pheobe Towne, they surrendered on the same day. Edmund officially gave his key and property to John Gould, an event Even (Evan) Morris and Thomas Perkins witnessed. It was confirmed by John Howe (brother-in-law to later accused Elizabeth Howe) that Edmund had sold his land to pay for his debts, of which there were a few owing money to John Gould and William Symonds, among others. Sarah likely watched as her husband did this, perhaps feeling humiliated as he had to give up everything because of his actions. Sarah possibly wondered if these hardships were just another test from God, to show devotion to her faith.

    The humiliated Bridges family packed their belongings and left Topsfield on a two-wheeled cart pulled by a horse. They were heading out and down the Ipswich Road into Salem Town, where Edmund used the money left over from his debt payments to buy some property near the Waterfront. He also built part of a wharf at the end of present-day Central St in Salem, near William Beckett, and got a license to sell alcohol in a Tavern. The small land was seen as an opportunity from God for the family of six, a new start for the family. A new town where they could benefit from the large community where it took more work to be noticed.

  Sadly, not many years after Sarah and Edmund's departure to Salem Town, Sarah's Father, William, passed away. There are no records to show the relationship between Sarah and her Father; the news of his death broke her heart. Being the youngest, Sarah likely held a special place in his heart, one would hope. Whether Sarah ever saw him again in the final two years of his life is unknown and lost to the historical record.

In Salem

  In Salem Town, Edumund built a home and barn on a small portion of land near the water on present-day Blaney St. Being a tavern, this once two-room home likely would've been expanded quickly. The rooms on the left-hand side of the house were used for the business: a lean-to, an extension in the back commonly used as a kitchen and taproom, and possibly a partitioned-off bedroom. The room in the front is used as the barroom to serve the food and drink to the customers. Above the barroom were more bedrooms for the guests, likely small partitioned-off rooms for overnight stays. The rest of the rooms on the right of the house were used by the Bridges Family for their day-to-day life, with the remaining room in the lean-to, first floor, and second floor as living areas.

The barn in the back was likely built for a dual purpose for the Tavern and the Bridges family's personal use: a barn, stables, chicken coop, swine sheds, and sheds used for day-to-day business. A garden was also likely available for the use of the Tavern, herbs such as lavender and rosemary for making the storage rooms fragrant; thyme, tarragon, and chives for giving flavor to the salads and rue, sage, and savory for giving flavor to the salads and vegetables. Mint for use with meat and drinks. Perhaps herbs like dill, lemon balm, coriander, and costmary were also grown in the Tavern for meals and flavoring liquors, such as costmary, to mark pages in the Bible by scent.

The fenced-in kitchen gardens likely were located in the rear closest to the kitchen, not necessarily organized by plant, but what grew where was known by Sarah. She would've tended to the other vegetables, such as leeks, onions, garlic, melons, English gourds, radishes, carrots, cabbages, and artichokes mixed with the herbs. Each would've been planted depending on the need for sun and water. A few fruit trees were grown over time, and the smaller property would've multiplied and was claustrophobic with the gardens, house, and various sheds in the rear. But its proximity would've made access easier for Sarah as she tended to the multiple meals she would've made in the kitchens.

However, being a smaller property in Salem Town limited the Bridges' production of crops and meats for the Tavern. A tavern with a larger property, such as the one run by John Proctor in Salem Farms, would've been able to feed his guests with everything from his farm. A tavern keeper in the Town, like Sarah and Edmund, would've relied on purchasing more meats, vegetables, and wood from those on large-scale farms to keep up with demand. However, having a Tavern in a place like Salem Town would've had more consistent customers and a more significant turnaround of guests. In contrast, a Tavern on the outskirts would've been except for those passing through seeking shelter.

     However, there were rules to abide by, such as not serving too much ale, leading to someone being publicly intoxicated, serving on the Sabbath, serving after 9 pm, or serving Quakers or Indigenous people. If the laws were broken, the tavern owners could be fined up to 10 shillings with additional fees between three to six shillings per additional offense seen by the court. If they concealed "drunken people" or allowed said person to appear in public drunk, they could be fined up to five pounds. Punishments such as standing in the stocks for up to three hours were given out on top of the fines to unruly tavern keepers and their patrons.

     Taverns were also prohibited from having their patrons play dice, cards, bowls, shuffleboard, and billiards. Guests participating in these acts could be fined six shillings and eight pence by the court if convicted or sent to jail. The Tavern-keepers could be fined up to forty shillings if convicted of a "gaming violation" in their tavern. Neighbors in Salem Village would be famous for such situations; the tavern run by Sarah and Edward Bishop would be well known for their loud guests, and unruly games would be made famous.

    Customers came and went; Sarah woke up early, with the smell of sea salt in the air, close to the South River. She was spending her day working hard in the kitchen to keep up with demand at the Tavern. Edmund helped, but considering he was also still working as an attorney in Salem Town, seeing that his other businesses were attended to, Sarah was likely left to tend to the needs of their patrons throughout the day. During this time, Edmund and Sarah only had their four young children, and between 1669 and 1677, they had no documented children or losses.

    As Salem Town grew, the merchant class developed through imported trade, including wines from Madeira and Canaries, enslaved people, among other goods. As the need for trade increased, the post-Stuart restoration English Parliament passed laws that made merchants pay tariffs on imports. These laws made colonists ship their imports to England and their final destination, creating an expensive and time-consuming process. Many merchants ignored this and sidestepped it with their West Indies and Barbados imports. The need for more exports resulted in the dwindling forest population as merchants needed wood for their ships, and a shipyard was near the home of the Bridges Tavern by 1700.

    A new Meeting House was built in 1672 in Salem Town. A rather large structure ordered by Edmund Batter, William Hathorne, father of John Hathorne, judge on the Court of Oyer and Terminer in 1692, William Browne Sr, and Capt. George Corwin, father of Johnathan Corwin, judge on the Court of Oyer and Terminer in 1692, for four hundred sixty-nine pounds and twelve shillings. The beams of the old Meeting House were put towards the construction of the new townhouse where a Latin school was held on the ground floor and court on the second. It was built in the center of Washington Street and would be the site of the many hearings Edmund and later the accused of the 1692 Outbreak were wrapped up in.

    Salem Town was busy, and Edmund worked hard as an attorney, trying to see himself climb the social ladder, much to the chagrin of his neighbors. Edmund's old habit of neighborly feuds returned in April 1678, and on the 20th of that month, Edmund went to court for a defamation case against Merchant Edmund Batter. Who was an apprentice of Edmund Batter was Samuel Sewall, who in 1692 would be on the Court of Oyer and Terminer and attend Sarah's examination in Salem Town. On April 20th, 1678, Edmund Batter accused Bridges of the following, stating that "*The plaintiff (Edmund Bridges) was the leader of a factious company in Salem and that it was their design to overthrow all order and government in the Town of Salem, also for saying the plaintiff (Bridges) was the cause of all mischief in Salem.*"

    Many of Sarah's family, came to Edmund's defense, including his brother-in-law Francis Nurse and Jacob Towne, as well as friends Jacob Hobb and Isaac Cooke. The men testified that they heard the false charges against him come from Edmund Batter and that, even in Topsfield, he was on the side of law and order. Sarah's nephew-in-law and husband of her niece Rebecca, Thomas Preston, testified that Edmund "*Never heard Bridges speak before he asked *leave of the moderator because he wished to prevent disorder."*

Jonathan Marston testified that Edmund Bridges "*Appeared turbulent, factious, and offensive, especially to Mr. Batter.*" He claimed that Bridges said, "*I know I stick in your eyes, I had rather stick in your throats,*" Another Merchant, Samuel Gardner Sr. testified that there was much disorder at local elections, with Henry West and William Dunton confirming that Edmund Bridges was the leader of a disorderly faction. Claiming Bridges stated, "*Do you think to make dogs of us? We will not be made dogs of,*" Bartholomew Gedney, a future judge on the Court of Oyer and Terminer, testified that he too agreed and stated Bridges had "*hindered the meeting and left the town without selectmen for the time,*"

Many people who spoke against him were of the merchant class or similarly wealthy men. The judges were Deputy Governor Samuel Symonds, Major General Daniel Denison, and Major William Hathorne, all merchants. This case pushed for merchants' voices to be heard in court as prior, they had difficulty getting their voices heard in the government. The court decided against Edmund Bridges, giving him a fine of two pounds, five shillings, and eight pence. Many people regardless spoke in Edmund Bridges' defense, including his family and Captain John Putnam, who himself and his family were having legal issues with the merchant class at the time. Ironically, some of the support of the Putnam disappeared by 1692, when his son, daughter-in-law, nephew, and grandniece became primary accusers against Sarah and her two sisters.

Capt. John Putnam and his wife signed a petition for Rebecca Nurse in 1692, alongside several other members of the Putnam family. Many familiar faces would pop up in the next few years, whether it was accusers, accused, or judges. Faces that Sarah would recognize in both the Court and Jails during Sarah's incarceration during the Trials. A moment in time that likely Sarah herself could've never predicted and showed the rather incestuous nature of the 1692 Salem Witch Trials.

Chapter 3
In the Year of 1678

The rest of 1678 was a bit bumpy for Sarah and her family; both husband and wife were in and out of Court for the remainder of 1678 regarding the strict tavern laws of the time. On June 25th, 1678, the Minister of the Salem Town Church, John Higginson, wrote a petition to the courts in Boston. He was complaining that several members of his community were operating illegal ordinaries and public drinking houses. He lists eighteen people in the Town of Salem and the nearby Village, many of whom would be involved in the later 1692 Outbreak.

"1. Mr (Bartholomew) Gedney, 2. Mr King, 3. Capt. More, 4. Ellin (Eleanor) Hollingwood (Hollingsworth), 5. Jo(hn) Proctor, 6. Nath(aniel) Ingersoll, 7. Darling, 8. Mr Croad, 9. Will(iam) Lake, 10. Edw(mund) Bridges, 11. Gilbert Taply, 12. Fra(ncis) Collins, 13. Goody Kippin, 14. Ruben Guppa, and that there are four more now at this time desire and endeavour to get appropbation or license, 15. John King, 16. John Pease, 17. Sam(uel) Eburn, 18. John Clifford. And being set in this place by God and men as a watchman by office, I dare not but discharge my duty in giving warning against the sin of drunkeness and the excessive number of drinking houses in this place."

    In the petition, Higginson believes that he must bring about illegal operations within his community. He goes on to mention Edmund specifically, "*And in particular you would not please license Edmund Bridges, he being not approved by the most of the sober people of this place, either for his sobriety or his fidelity to law and good order,*" The final comment of Edmund's "fidelity" to law and order is similar to those that had defended and accused him in his April case against Edmund Batter. Whether Higginson was present is unknown, but as the local Minister, his knowledge of the event was prevalent. Higginson likely supported Batter and the powerful Merchants who spoke against Bridges in the case. How Sarah and

Edmund felt at this accusation from their Minister is unknown, but one can likely conclude it wouldn't make Sunday services comfortable. This would parallel events in fifteen years with the Reverend Samuel Parris and the events of 1692-1693.

In the same Petition, James Smith, William Smith, Richard Palmer, John Bolorig, and Thomas Coates confirmed purchasing cider from the Bridges' Tavern. William Smith and Richard Palmer testified that they bought three quarts of cider two months prior and then four quarts three weeks before, with James Shaw testifying he paid 3 pence per quart of cider. John Bolorig and Thomas Coates stated that "*Last Sabbath day around seven at night,*" purchased a quart of cider, and "*His girl or the maid brought it,*" likely referring to his daughters Mary or Hannah as they were about 11 and 8 years old respectively.

William Smith was found to have been drunk, confirmed by Henry West, who witnessed his drunkenness and abusive nature to a tithingman. William confessed and stated he had five quarts of cider at Edmund Bridges's home. On May 15th, he was fined, and Edmund himself was made to be brought to Court for "*retailing cider within doors contrary to law, whereby one was found drunk.*" Francis Nurse and Christopher Lattamore made assure that Edmund would appear at the next court session regarding the case.

    The case seems to have been dismissed, with the record stating, "*Edmund Bridges presented for affirming an untruth or lie several times, was dismissed, it not being legally proven,*" John Putnam, John Pickering Sr, and Manases Mastone were present as witnesses, but no testimony from them survives. Sarah also appears in a record alongside her husband, testifying that they saw Henry West and John Norton speak fallacious language. It's ironic since Henry West was the one who saw William Smith speak abusive language to a tithingman.

    For once, Sarah could breathe as Edmund could do his job as an attorney in a case between John Proctor and Giles Corey of Salem Farms. John Proctor accused Giles of "willfully" attempting to burn down his house; Giles countered and sued John for this. Many people, including Giles's wife, confirmed they had seen the fire and the damage it did. However, it was not Giles who caused the act; in fact, James Poland testified that he saw John Proctor tell his son that he had brought a lamp into the room. Then, after he set it near some boards, the fire ignited Jane and Caleb Moore affirmed. The Court sided with Giles Corey and was dismissed as a result; who would know that within the next fourteen years, both men and their wives would find themselves imprisoned on charges of Witchcraft?

    Edmund continued his work as an attorney during the summer of 1678, with Sarah even testifying against a patron from their tavern. When Quaker Charles Hill had asked for some ale and cake, Sarah and Edmund stated he must go to Meeting. He responded that he had already gone to Quaker Meeting as he scorned going to the "old Higginson" services and claimed that the Reverend John Higginson was "an oppressor of the poor." That same summer, Edmund went to Court again, this time for his unfaithfulness as an attorney for Benjamin Mazure, whose Edmund worked for prior.

    Jersyman, Phillip English (formerly L'Anglois) came to Edmund's defense, and as a result, Edmund no longer was an attorney for Mazure. But he became one for Phillip English; this action angered the Merchants of Salem Town as Phillip was a French Anglican. A "new wave" of Frenchmen had begun to settle in Salem after his arrival. Edmund, who had already angered the merchants from prior encounters, expressed his fondness for dressing out of his station. He likely developed a tremendous big red target on his back from his association with Phillip English.

  Sarah appears to testify alongside her husband in a few cases in 1678 but remains out of the historical narrative until 1692. Her thoughts and feelings are lost moments like this, likely made her angry; reminding her of what happened in the case of John Gould, where they had to give up their land to settle their debts and relocate to Salem Town. From here, there was nowhere else to go for the Bridges family likely, thought Sarah; one could only imagine her praying that he would do something to end it.

  The following year, Edmund, in addition to his actions as an attorney, was in Court for swearing, testifying against a woman who had an affair, and wearing a

Periwig. The latter was blasphemous as it switched gender roles and was not fashionable in the eyes of the Court. This isn't the first recorded instance of someone breaking the set Fashion Laws; people wearing silk hoods, wools, and other fabrics and trims are recorded in the *Essex County Quarterly Courts*.

1679

1679 began with the public humiliation of Bridget Oliver; a few months prior, she publicly argued with her husband, Thomas Oliver. Calling him "*An old rouge*" and an "*A devil,*" both were brought to Court on the condition that they'd be let go pending a payment of a fine. Thomas's daughter paid for his, leaving Bridget to stand alone before the Court and was bound and gagged with her offense pinned to her cap. She stood in the cold January air before the Meeting House in the town square and well as Minister John Higginson preached his sermon on Lecture Day. One has to wonder if Sarah witnessed this event and if, in late May 1692, she recognized this woman who would join her and her sisters in the Boston Jail.

Sarah again appears in court records in April of 1679 as a witness in the case of Thomas Maul v. James Brown. Thomas Maul claims that Sgt. James Brown had "*Bragged that he could open the door with a cold chisel,*" and Maul's shop was broken into that night. Maul immediately suspected James and reported it to the authorities, with many people, including Sarah, Edmund, and Maul's wife Naomi, who testified that in one way or another, they heard Brown's remark and agreed that he had been the one to do it. There is no record of James Brown's punishment, but it was likely a fine or a set jail incarceration.

But, all was not lost for the Bridges Family; in May of 1679, Sarah and Edmund were given new seats in the Meeting House despite the apparent dislike of them from the Reverend Higginson. Sarah was seated in the women's pews with her sister Rebecca and Elizabeth (nee Bassett) Proctor. Edmund was moved to a galley seat belonging to the deceased Sargent Lake, further away from the Reverend John Higginson. Merchants and the Minister still glared daggers at Edmund Bridges, a feeling Sarah felt as whispers could've passed her in the streets of the Town. Even the new assistant Minister Nicolas Noyes, aged thirty-two, joined his superior on the hatred of periwigs, writing an essay entitled "*An Essay Against Periwigs*" in 1702.

"*Removeth one notable, visible distinction of sex,*"

Chapter 4
Goodwife Cloyse, formerly Bridges

Edmund and Sarah did their duties; Edmund had his job as an attorney until June 11th, 1680. Several unknown "*considerable persons*" complained against Edmund in Court, stating that,

> "*Complaining that he was a disturber of the peace and quiet of the town, and promoter and manager of unrighteous and vexatious suits, and laboring to make factions in town meetings; and after notice and hearing, the court ordered that he should not plead any cause in any civil proceeding, but his own, and should be debarred from voting in town affairs, and incapable of bearing any civil or military office in Salem, during the pleasure of the court.*"

Edmund was officially and legally disbarred and fell into some "bodily affliction." He had missed a few court hearings and was brought to court to explain his absences. We don't know what his illness was; it killed him quickly, perhaps Tuberculosis or some other disease. His and Sarah's eldest son had married a woman named Elizabeth Croade, and upon that marriage, Edmund sold his share of his wharf to his son. Sadly, death would hit Sarah hard from the Summer of 1682 into the Winter of 1683. On June 24th, 1682, their eldest child, Edmund III, died, survived by his wife and their posthumous son, born after his death, also named Edmund.

By September 1682, Edmund died; his death date was not recorded. They had been married for twenty-two years. As with anything, Sarah could've been overwhelmed with grief, regardless of the challenges he put her through during their marriage. He still worked to provide for his family, and every mistake he made was for the benefit of his family. He left the small property and wharf in Salem to his son Edmund. But as his son was dead, the estate passed to his daughter-in-law and his posthumously born grandson of the same name who died after birth.

Sarah was left homeless and within a week or so of his death, Sarah and her four surviving children between the ages of two and eighteen returned to Topsfield. Her arrival did not last long, and on September 12th, Sarah was ordered out of the town by the Constable. None of Sarah's family took her in; her brothers Jacob and Joseph and her sister Mary lived in town. Her brother Edmund died in 1678, but his wife hadn't (and never did) remarry and was alone with nine children. Her mother, Joanna, was presumably still alive by the time Sarah returned, but none of them offered a helping hand of "good charity." It seems as if the family did not want to help Sarah and her children, but most likely, they were unable to help Sarah. Adding five mouths to large families would've been hard for anyone to maintain.

  Sarah left, holding her young daughter Abigail, and her other three children followed behind her. Their fates were uncertain; without a home, Sarah marched out of Topsfield, putting her faith in God, who had made him guide her. If her mother was alive, she passed not long after; Sarah lost another parent, never seeing her again. The estate was divided between the sons, and the personal effects were divided between the three daughters, Sarah, Mary, and Rebecca. Each child signed their mark with an "X," and at the time, Sarah was still "Sarah Bridges," but within a few weeks, at least one of her prayers would be answered. Sarah was no longer Sarah Bridges but became "Sarah Cloyse."

~~~

  Peter and Edmund Bridges were familiar with one another, having at least taken inventory of the estate of Richard Cranvier. Whether they were friends is unknown, but by 1683, the couple was wed; it's likely within weeks of Sarah signing the will of William and Joanna. Where Sarah went with five children during that time is unknown; perhaps she had found someone to take her in. But no records survive of where Sarah went, but Sarah's situation improved regardless. By late August of 1683, Sarah had given birth to a son named Benoni. Sadly, the child died not long after birth; he was baptized on September 2nd.
  Peter Cloyse was born May 27th, 1639, son of John and Abigail Cloyse of Watertown, Massachusetts. He was the

second child with an elder brother named John and younger siblings Nathaniel, Abigail, and Thomas. His mother, Abigail, died at some point before 1656 and remarried to a woman named Jane; her maiden name was lost to history. The Cloyse family was comfortable, in 1656 John Sr. sold his house and land to Samuel Stratton for thirty pounds, stating, "*Where my late mansion house was by God's providence burnt down.*" Mansion houses in the 17th Century were seen as four-room homes or more, such as the Corwin and Turner-Ingersoll House.

By 1660, the Cloyse family moved North to Wells, in present day Maine, where Peter married his first wife, Hannah, in 1664. The couple remained in Wells and had five children between 1664 and 1678: Sarah (1666), Hannah (1667), Peter (1668), Mary (1674), and James (1678). After the birth of their son James, the couple sold their land in Maine and returned to Salem. There, Peter became a member of the Salem Town Church. Sadly, Hannah passed the following year in 1680, leaving Peter alone with five children, financially though Peter was better off than his future wife Sarah.

Sarah and Peter Cloyse became tenant farmers living on property owned by Daniel Andrews in Salem Village. The couple and their ten combined children aged eighteen to two. As Peter was a bit more financially well off, perhaps the couple lived in a two-room home with a lean-to in the back. Their neighbor was George Jacobs Jr, whose father, George Jacobs Sr, occupied the land on which Sarah was born in the Northfields portion of Salem. Peter provided a decently simple life for Sarah and their family; he did his work as a farmer, and Sarah did her work in the house.

    The antics of her marriage to Edmund were long gone; Sarah and Peter did the routine of work, Church, and sleep. By 1685, Sarah gave birth to her final child, Hepzibah, when she was forty-three years old. The occupants of the Cloyse home dwindled when Peter's daughters Hannah and Sarah married husbands of their own in 1686 and 1689; her son Benjamin married Elizabeth Haven in 1689. On August 3rd, 1685, Peter joined Captain Richard Leach, Lieutenant John Putnam, Sargent. John Leach, Jacob Barney, Joshua Ree, Jeremey Watts, Jonathan Putnam, Edward Bishop Jr,

Thomas Rainment, and Isreal Porter to investigate the death of his neighbor, George Jacobs Jr.'s daughter Mary Jacobs. She had died only a few months prior, with the group finding that she had fallen into the well and drowned.

~~~

    Within three years of Sarah's marriage to Peter in 1686, the Massachusetts Bay Colony Charter was revoked by Parliament. The new regime of James II of England had spread to the colonies, and one of those ways was to force the ideals of the Church of England onto the Puritan colonists of New England. Edmund Andros was appointed Governor of the Dominion and was deeply unpopular with most of the population due. Laws were passed challenging the right of the colonists to own their land; most of these laws were passed to increase tax revenue. By early 1688, the King was overthrown by his daughter and her husband during the Glorious Revolution.
    During the remaining months of the Andros government of Massachusetts Bay,

in November of 1688, word spread to the Towns and Villages in the Massachusetts Bay Colony of the hanging of the Catholic Goodwife Glover. She had been accused of afflicting the four children of John Goodwin, sending them into fits and strange symptoms. After some time, the children named her as their affliction; it's said that the symptoms began after Goodwife Glover argued with the elder of the Goodwin children. She was arrested, tried, and sentenced to hang on November 16th, 1688. Goodwife Glover was the first person hanged in thirty-two years and the first person convicted in nine years for the crime of Witchcraft.

    Many of the Goodwin children's symptoms mirrored those afflicted in 1692 according to; Cotton Mather would go on to write *Memorable Provinces*. Which entailed the course of events, including Mather's own opinions of Goodwife Glover. These events were even recorded by Samuel Sewall in his diary, describing Glover's execution on the Boston Neck Gallows. It's probable she was targeted due to her Catholic beliefs and would go on to become a martyr in the centuries following her execution, but her conviction remains to this day. She is one of eight people who have not been cleared of the capital crime of Witchcraft in the state of Massachusetts.

    On April 18th, 1689, the people of Boston revolted against Andros, and he was imprisoned alongside his supporters because of his unpopular laws. His government quickly collapsed, sending the colony into legal limbo and falling under the de facto leadership of Simon Bradstreet. King William's War broke out during this time as well, seeing fighting between the Colonists the French and the Indigenous nations. As a result, the taxes, war, and defense hit the economy hard, and the colony had difficulty rebuilding its trade. Soon, Increase Mather, father of Cotton Mather, would venture to England to secure the charter for the New Colony.

~~~

    Despite the hardships around them, the family pushed through, and through Peter, Sarah began to elevate herself socially within the community. 1689 Samuel Parris, a failed merchant and plantation owner, turned minister and replaced Deodat Lawson as the village minister. While Sarah and Peter lived quaintly on their farm, the village around them was largely discontented, struggling to keep a permanent Minister since they were allowed to build their own Meeting House in 1672. He was ordained, but his delay in his acceptance of the position and disputes on salary angered many of the Village's members. Ironically, Peter was one of his supporters not knowing how quickly things would change within the next five years.

But, under Parris's leadership, on January 6th, 1690, Sarah became a covenant member of the Salem Village Church, joining her husband and sisters. Soon, things would sour in the village; in 1691, community members began to not pay his salary. This is a tactic that the villagers have used on previous Ministers, such as George Burroughs, in an attempt to get him to leave. Whether Sarah and Peter were of this group is unknown, but as soon as the end of 1691 turned into the cold winter of January 1692. Between local political tensions within the Village and the Town, the ongoing threat of the French and Indigenous people, illness spreading like wildfire would ignite the oncoming wildfire. There was no one thing or person to blame for the coming events of the new year.

Part 2:
January 1692-April 1692

Chapter 5
The Devil Comes to Salem Village

January 1692

The year began with cold, wet weather and heavy snowfall throughout January. Legends would develop in the 330 years since that it was during this time the young girls of Salem Village would sit before Tituba, the Indigenous person enslaved by Reverend Parris. Learning different forms of Voodoo that would later cause these girls "afflictions." These theories wrongfully blame Tituba for the cause of the Witch Trials; no reason has been proven. Voodoo perpetuated since the 19th century were actually forms of English folk magic, moldy bread since the 1970s, or "land grab" since the 1950s, have been proven not to have been the cause of the outbreak. Instead, it was a whole cluster that fell into the perfect storm.

The colony lost its charter a few years back, and Increase Mather, father of the minister Cotton Mather, had been in England for the past four years settling on a new charter. His efforts were successful in getting Sir William Phips the position as the new governor, and the two men were so grateful that they kissed King William III's hand in thanks. The villagers went about their usual business in the winter. However, something dark lurked amongst the storms. Soon, in the household of the Reverend Samuel Parris, alongside his wife Elizabeth; two daughters, Susannah, and Elizabeth "Betty"; son Thomas; ward Abigail; and two enslaved people, Tituba and John Indian would come into chaos.

    Betty and Abigail had begun to convulse and writhe in their beds, claiming that something was harming them. An unseen force visible only to the eyes of Betty and Abgail, the specters bit and choked the two girls night and day. They barked like dogs, flapped their arms as if they were birds and attempted to jump into the hearth to escape the specters. People in the 17th Century believed that a Witch had the power to send an apparition that looked and sounded like them. To anywhere they wanted to harm anyone they chose, who could only be seen by who the Witch wanted. The population also believed that God would never allow an innocent person to do such a thing. Only when someone gave consent to the Devil was something like this possible.

February 1692

February would only worsen things in the home of Reverend Samuel Parris, Sarah Good, a homeless beggar woman who often cursed those who refused to give her charity. Sarah Good wandered the streets of Salem Village with her four-year-old daughter, Dorothy, and an unnamed infant, sleeping in barns while her husband, William Good, attempted to make a living. She came to the parsonage early in the month asking for good charity for herself and her daughter Dorothy. Samuel did not give to Sarah but gave a bit of food to her young daughter. Sarah thanked him for giving to her daughter and walked away, and according to Reverend Parris, she muttered as she walked away. Betty and Abigail fell into fits almost immediately after Sarah left the parsonage. While things worsened in the household of

Reverend Samuel Parris, a copy of the new Charter arrived in Boston; it seemed things were beginning to look up for the Massachusetts Bay Colony.

In Salem Village, John Putnam Jr and his wife Hannah welcomed a newborn daughter on February 15th. Sadly, within eight weeks, the child would die, a victim of the high child mortality rate of colonial America. Soon, other people in the Village showed signs of affliction similar to those of Betty Parris, Abigail Williams, and Ann Putnam Jr, eldest daughter of Thomas and Ann Putnam. On the 24th, Dr. William Griggs examined Betty and Abigail, concluding they were *under an evil hand,* The next day, the Reverend and his wife left to attend a Thursday lecture in a neighboring town where Reverend Parris have the opportunity to get a second opinion on the ongoing issues in the Village.

Mary Sibley, a nearby neighbor, instructed Tituba and her husband, John Indian, on how to help the two girls: a witch cake. Tituba was told to retrieve the urine of Betty and Abigail and then mix it with a rye meal to bake it into a loaf of bread. The final step was to feed it to the family dog; this would then harm the witch, afflicting them and possibly revealing the witch, or so they believed. Parris and his wife Elizabeth returned to the Parsonage, and the girls were worse off than when they left. Upon discovering the witch cake, Parris beats Tituba, angered at bringing such things into his home.

    Other ministers believed that before, the girls could not see who was afflicting them. After the dog consumed the witch cake, the girls' eyes were opened to the evils of the invisible world. It allowed them to see who was now harming and causing their misfortune. Now, more girls are claiming to be abused by specters, including Ann Putnam Jr and Dr. William Griggs's niece, Elizabeth Hubbard.

    On the 26th, Betty and Abigail officially named Tituba the one causing their pain. Claiming that her specter was pursuing them from about the room, their epileptic fits grew worse. Their bodies would contort unnaturally, bewildering the frightened Reverend and his wife. They struggled to breathe as if the invisible specters were choking the young girls. They asked the girls who were doing this to them, and the girls did name people, names of people who were the "usual suspects."

Their symptoms matched those of the Goodwin children, afflicted by the Irish Servant "Goody Glover" in 1688. It was a recent case in Boston only four years ago; Cotton Mather reported it in his book Memorable Provinces, written only a year after the event in 1689. To get a second opinion, Parris invited other local ministers and gentlemen to witness the violent fits of the girls. The Reverend John Hale of Beverly wrote, "*Had enquired diligently into the sufferings of the afflicted, concluded they were supernatural and feared the hand of Satan was upon them,*" Parris was advised to keep praying for the girls; they also interrogated Tituba to hopefully discover the truth behind everything.

Tituba did admit to making the witch cake, claiming that her previous owner in Barbados was a witch and had taught her methods of countermagic. But Tituba stated her innocence then and did not name Mary Sibley as the one who instructed her to make the cake. As the problems grew in the Parris household, they worsened elsewhere; Ann Putnam Jr officially named Sarah Good their afflicter. Elizabeth Hubbard, who was running an errand for her family, claimed she was stalked by a wolf that had either been sent by Sarah Good or was Sarah Good after she transformed herself.

Elizabeth Hubbard further claimed that night she was harassed in her home by the specter of Sarah Osbourne. Around eighteen years prior, the then Sarah Prince defied expectations when she went against the terms of her husband's will by denying her son's inheritance. Sarah had overtaken her husband's 150-acre farm and kept it for herself and her new husband. A man named Alexander Osbourne, a former entrepreneur whose indenture Sarah paid off using money she got from her husband's will. On top of the girl's fits and convulsions, the terrible weather did not help either, likely keeping many up through the night with heavy winds and rains, which lasted into February 29th. Due to the girl's worsening condition during the Sabbath on the 28th, four men took matters into their own hands and braved the elements. Despite the nasty weather flooding the roads and making the almost 5-mile walk impossible.

Thomas Putnam, father of Ann Putnam; his brother, Edward Putnam; Joseph Hutchinson; and Thomas Preston, son-in-law of Rebecca Nurse and nephew-in-law of Sarah Cloyse, filed the first legal complaint against Tituba, Sarah Good, and Sarah Osbourne. At that moment, Thomas Preston likely never knew how the oncoming outbreak would affect his family. Every family, including those that would become primary accusers like the Putnam's, Walcott's, and Pope's, and the accused like the Nurse's, Cloyse's, and Esty's, couldn't have seen what would come. By the end of the day, Sarah Good, Tituba, and Sarah Osbourne would all be apprehended and made to wait at Ingersoll's Tavern to await their examinations.

March 1692

The Month of March began with clearer weather and three Witchcraft Examinations. A witchcraft accusation was not as common as most would think in 17th-century Massachusetts. It was challenging to get the complaint issued, and it was difficult for it to go from a hearing to a formal trial. Two witnesses to the same event were commonly needed for the verdict to proceed to a trial. Most cases were found to have been not guilty, and even before the 1688 case of Goody Glover, two people were convicted, but both had their convictions overturned.

The proceedings were initially to be held at Ingersoll's Ordinary, where the accused were already held to await the examination. However, because of the large crowds, they had to move their examinations to the more significant Meeting House not far down the road. Each of them was interrogated one by one, beginning with Sarah Good, whom John Hathorne questioned.

"Sarah Good, what evil spirit have you familiarity with?" asked Hathorne

"None," replied Sarah

"Have you made no contract with the Devil?" questioned Hathorne.

"No," stated Sarah.

"Why do you hurt these children?" asked Hathorne.

"I do not hurt them; I scorn it," affirmed Sarah.

Sarah Good continued denying the accusations; when asked about her visit to the Parsonage and the "muttering" that followed, she merely thanked Parris's good charity towards her daughter. When asked why she tormented the girls, she responded, "*I do not know, but it was some you brought into the meeting house with you,*" Hathorne pointed out she was the only one of the three in the Meeting House. Still, Sarah responded, "*But you brought in two more,*" Hathorne asked who it was then out of the other two that hurt the girls, and Sarah answered, "It was Osbourne." Sarah then asked to recite her Commandments and was asked who she served, to which she replied, "*The God that made heaven and earth.*" Her manner during her examination was described as "Spiteful manner," and even her husband was asked if she was a witch, to which he thought that if she weren't one, she very soon would be one.

~~~

Up next was Sarah Osbourne, who, when Hathorne asked her if she was familiar with the Devil, replied, "*None.*" When asked if she had made contact with the Devil, she replied, "*No, I never saw the Devil in my life."* Hathorne then asked if she was familiar with Sarah Good, who had accused her of Witchcraft only a moment ago, unbeknownst to Osbourne.

"What familiarity have you with Sarah Good," questioned Hathorne.

"None. I have not seen her these two years,"

"Where did you see her then,"

"One day, going to Town,"

"What communications had you with her?"

"I had none, only how do you do or so, I did not know her by name,"

"What did you call her then?

"Sarah Good say that it was you that hurt the children,"

"I do not know that the devil goes about in my likeness to do any hurt."

Hathorne then asked the girls present to stand and look at Sarah Osbourne to see if they could confirm it was Osbourne. To which they confirmed, stating that they had seen her in this very habit (clothing) she was now in. Sarah then remarked that she was more likely to be bewitched than be a witch, to which Hathorne asked what she meant by it. Sarah then described how *"She was frightened one time in her sleep and either saw or dreamed that she saw a thing like an Indian all black which did pinch her in her neck and pulled her by the back part of her head to the door of the house."*

She was asked if that spirit or any other spirits presented themselves to her, to which she replied, "No."

"What lying spirit was it then."

"It was a voice that I thought I heard,"

"What did it propound to you?"

"That I should go no more to meeting, but I said I would and did go the next Sabbath day,"

"Were you never tempted further?"

"No,"

"Why did you yield thus far to the devil as never to go to meeting since?"

"Alas, I have been sick," she said, further mentioning she couldn't go with her husband. Others said she had not been at Meeting this "year and two months."

~~~

The last to be brought in was Tituba. Hathorne began his line of questioning with,

"Tituba, what evil spirit are you familiar with?"

"None," replied Tituba

"Why do you hurt these children?" asked Hathorne

"I do not hurt them," stated Tituba

"Who is it then?" inquired Hathorne

"The devil for ought I know,"

"Did you never see the devil?"

"The devil came to me and bid me serve him," described Tituba

"Who have you seen?" asked Hathorne.

"Four women and sometimes hurt the children,"

"Who were they?"

"Goody Osbourne and Sarah Good, and I do not know who the other was Sarah Good and Osbourne would have me hurt the children, but I would not further say there was a Tall Man of Boston that she did see,"

"When did you see them?"

"Last night at Boston,"

"What did they say to you when they said hurt the children? And did you hurt them, no?"

"No, there are four women and one man. They hurt the children and then lay all upon me, and they tell me if I will not hurt the children, they will hurt me," Referring to the almost supposed month where she was accosted by the various specters forcing her to hurt the girls.

"But did you not hurt them?"

"Yes, but I will hurt them no more,"

"Are you not sorry that you did hurt them?"

"Yes,"

"And why, then, do you hurt them?"

"They say hurt children, or we will do worse to you,"

"What have you seen a man come to me and say, serve me? What service?"

"Hurt the children, and last night there was an appearance that said kill the children, and if I did not go on hurting the children, they would do worse to me,"

"What is this appearance do you see?"

"Sometimes it is like a hog and sometimes like a great dog," Tituba would go on to say she had seen this spectral dog four more times.

"What did it say to you?"

"The black dog said serve me, but I said I am afraid. He said if I did not, he would do worse to me,"

"What did you say to it?"

"I will serve you no longer than he said he would hurt me, and then he looked like a man and threatened to hurt me. She said that this man had a yellow bird that he kept with him, and he told me he had more pretty things that he would give me if I would serve him,"

"What were these pretty things?"

"He did not show me them,"

"What else have you seen?"

"Two cats, a red cat and a black cat,"

"What did they say to you?"

"They said serve me,"

"When did you see them last?"

"Last night, they said to serve me, but I said I would not,"

"What service?"

"She said hurt the children,"

"Did you not pinch Elizabeth Hubbard this morning?"

"The man brought her to me and made me pinch her,"

"Why did you go to Thomas Putnam's last night and hurt his child?"

"They pull and had me and make go,"

"And what would have you do?"

"Kill her with a knife,"

Lt. Thomas Fuller, a man of seventy-four years stood and confirmed that he had heard of Ann Putnams complaints. Stating that the girls' heads were going to cut off by the specters.

"How did you go?"

"We ride upon sticks and are there presently,"

"Do you go through the trees or over them?"

"We see nothing but are there presently,"

"Why did you not tell your master?"

"I was afraid they said they would cut off my head if I told,"

"Would you not have hurt others if you could,"

"They said they would hurt others, but they could not,"

"What attendants?"

"A yellow bird, and she would have given me one,"

"What meat did she give it?"

"It did suck her between her fingers,"

"Did not you hurt Mr Corwin's child?"

"Goody Good and Goody Osbourne

told me that they did hurt Mr. Corwin's child and would have had me hurt him too, but I did not,"

"What had Sarah Osbourne?"

"Yesterday she had a thing with a head like a woman with legs and wings, Abigail Williams went onto describe that the same creature with the head of Sarah Osbourne yesterday then turned into the shape of Osbourne.

"What else have you seen with Goody Osbourne?"

"Another thing is hairy; it goes upright like a man. It hath only two legs,"

"Did you not see Sarah Good upon Elizabeth Hubbard last Saturday,"

"I did see her set a wolf upon her to afflict her,"

The group of afflicted affirmed Tituba's statement of Sarah Good's spectral wolf going after Elizabeth Hubbard.

"What clothes doth the man we go in?"

"He goes in black clothes, a tall man with white hair, I think,"

"How doth the woman go?"

"In a white hood and a black hood with a top knot,"

"Do you see who it is that torments these children now?"

"Yes, it is Goody Good. She hurts them in her shape,"

"And who is it that hurts them now?"

"I am blind now; I cannot see,"

At that moment, Tituba's examination ended, claiming that the angry specters of Osbourne and Good blinded her. The crowded Meeting House grew panicked, frightened over Tituba's detailed confession. The next day, Tituba was examined for a second time. There, she states she saw nine marks (names) written in the Devil's book. Whether Sarah and her husband Peter were in attendance is unknown, but if they were. Would they have known how this confession would spiral into nine months of pain and fear for Sarah Cloyse and her sisters?

Chapter 6
Innocent as the Child Unborn

March 1692

    Sarah's initial thoughts at the beginning of the proceedings are unknown; she likely knew of the whispers against Tituba, Sarah Good, and Sarah Osbourne. But whether she knew of whispers against other people is unknown. Martha Corey was suspected since the 12th after she knew Edward Putnam, the Uncle of Ann Putnam Jr., and Ezekiel Cheever came to visit her to "See what clothes she had on." The next day, a new specter visited and began to torment Ann Putnam Jr and eventually her mother, Ann Putnam Sr. At first, the specter, clad only in a shift and the nightcap, sat in a chair belonging to Ann Putnam Jr's grandmother. Remaining unidentified, Ann's Mother and the maidservant, Mercy Lewis. The two women began listing names of possible women who went to services with them.

    Mercy Lewis was about eighteen in 1692 and a survivor of two raids in present-day Maine. Mercy was also the niece by marriage to Sarah Cloyse. Mercy's Aunt, Susannah Lewis, married Thomas Cloyse, brother of Peter Cloyse. Mercy never directly implicated Sarah during the Witch Trials; instead, she accused her sisters, Rebecca Nurse and Mary Esty.

On Rebecca's June 3rd grand jury, Ann Jr claimed, "*I did not know her name then: though I knew where she used to sit in our Meeting house.*" Who put the name "Goody Nurse" in Ann's mind is unknown; when her son Samuel and son-in-law John visited the Putnam household, Mercy and Goody Putnam had a back and forth about whether or not it was the other who said it was Rebecca. The real Rebecca Nurse was ill with a unknown ailment when the specter was identified. She was rendered for what would be the final weeks in her home.

Word traveled fast to everyone but Rebecca; Sarah herself would've been shocked at her sister's accusation. Being the youngest of the Towne siblings, Sarah did not grow up with Rebecca, as Rebecca was married by 1644 when Sarah was two. But Rebecca and Francis did support Sarah in times of need, with Francis attesting to her first husband, Edmund Bridges Jr, good behavior in a 1678 slander case against Edmund Batter. The two sisters likely saw each other weekly when attending Salem Village Meeting House services. When Sarah lived in Salem Town during her first marriage, Rebecca was a covenant member of the Salem Town Church.

  No primary records attesting to their relationship, but it can be assumed that it was at least amicable and that the two cared for one another. Perhaps it was Sarah who had Peter join his landlord, Daniel Andrew, his brother-in-law, Israel Porter, and his wife, Elizabeth, on a visit to Rebecca's home on March 22. Sarah likely grew worried after Martha Corey's arrest. Martha, unlike the first three accused, was a covenant member of the Salem Village Church. While she was a decently respected woman whose arrest and accusation did not shock anyone due to her scandalous past.

  Martha, either after her first marriage to Henry Rich or before her marriage to Giles, produced a mixed-race son who was mixed race and lived with her son in the home of John Clifford in Salem Town. Martha also had another son named Thomas, who was around fifteen years old in 1692, when he was possibly baptized at the Salem Village Church after his mother's confirmation in April 1690. However, to join the Church, one must confess all one's sins and be voted in by other covenant members. So, others likely saw Martha as someone trying to "fix her life" by becoming respectable.

However, Rebecca did not have a shameful past; she was widely respected, as was her husband and family. She, too, was a covenant member of the Salem Town Church and was among "the Chosen" for a place in Heaven. Sarah knew of all this, was likely concerned for her sister's safety and by having her sister named, she wanted something done before her sister ended up like Martha. So, Peter joined Daniel Andrews, Israel Porter, and his wife Elizabeth on March 22, 1692. They arrived at the Nurse Homestead, a small two-room house with a hall and hall chamber above, sitting on three hundred acres of land. Being ill, Rebecca likely slept on the main floor in a hinged bed, an item used for guests' arrival.

Dressed in a cap, shift, and possibly a robe for more modesty and layers of wool blankets above her, she lay there, likely surprised at the visit of her brother-in-law and friends. The visiting group sat at her bedside, discussing how Rebecca was feeling due to her illness at the time. She described her condition as "weak and low," having felt this way for almost a week with an unknown illness. Rebecca, however, felt blessed, feeling that she had more of the Lord in her presence now than she had when she wasn't sick. To the surprise of the visiting group, Rebecca changed the conversation to the recent ongoing events in the Village.

Rebecca had grieved for them, praying that their afflictions be cured. Still, she could not visit them as she did, too. *"Reason of fits that she formerly used to have for people said it was awful to behold,"* Mentioning. However, she believed some of the accused were innocent of the crimes they were accused of, but the document does not mention *which* of the accused she believed were innocent. The visiting group then took the opportunity that Rebecca herself had been named. Rebecca responded, *"If it be so, the will of the Lord be done."* But still sat there still and amazed at her accusation, and added, "*I am innocent as the child unborn, but surely what sine hath God found out in me unrepented of that he should lay such an affliction upon me in my old age.*" The group sat alongside Rebecca, feeling their friend's shock. Believing her reaction was genuine as they could not discern whether or not she had heard of anything prior.

      The day after Peter Cloyse visited his ailing sister-in-law, Jonathan and Edward Putnam made the trip to Salem Town to file a complaint against Rebecca Nurse. The complaint dictated that she be brought to the home of Lieutenant Nathaniel Ingersoll pending her Examination. A complaint against the young daughter of Sarah Good, four-year-old Dorothy Good, was also filed on this day. Adding two more people to the ongoing Witch Hunt, did the Magistrates surmise that these two more names of the nine in the Devil's Book, mentioned by Tituba at her second Examination?

The Warrant of the Apprehension of Rebecca Nurse

~~~

March 23, 1692

To the Marshall of Essex or his deputy
There being complaint this day made before us by Edward Putnam and Jonathan Putnam Yeomen, both of Salem Village, against Rebecca Nurse, the wife of Francis Nurse of Salem Village, for vehement suspicion of having committed sundry acts of witchcraft and thereby having done much hurt and injury to the bodies of Ann Putnam the wife of Thomas Putnam of Salem Village Anna Putnam the daughter of said Thomas Putnam and Abigail Williams &etc

You are, therefore, in their Majesties names, hereby required to apprehend and bring before us Rebecca Nurse, the wife of Francis Nurse of Salem Village, tomorrow at about Eight of the Clock in the forenoon at the house of Lt Nathaniell Ingersoll in Salem Village in order to her Examination Relating to the aboves'd premises and hereof you are not to fail Salem March the 23'd 1691/2

per us *John. Hathorne] Assists

*Jonathan Corwin] Assists

*March 24'th, 1691/2 I have apprehended the body of Rebecca Nurse and brought her to the house of Le't Nath. Ingersoll, where she is in Custody
per *George Herrick
Marshall of Essex*

~~~

March 24th began early for the Nurse family when the Marshall of Essex County arrived at the door to the Nurse's Home. The presence of the Marshall likely surprised the Nurses when, upon hearing the warrant, it was read out loud for all to hear. The seventy-one-year-old Rebecca was ushered out of her warm bed, likely hastily dressed as she would've been in her shift. Her hands were tied, and she was brought out of her home for the last time. She was brought to Ingersoll's Ordinary and kept in an upstairs room for two hours before her examination.

It's not recorded that Sarah was present at her sister's examination; however, it was common for the family to attend their loved one's examinations. Sarah and Peter lived less than an hour's walk from the Meeting House, which would've been enough time for one of Sarah's nephews to make his way from the Nurse Farm up to their home and for them to return to the Village Center. Sarah, much like her brother-in-law and his children, would've felt feelings of anger and confusion at the site of learning of her sister's arrest.

The Meeting House would've filled quickly upon word of Rebecca's Examination; if she had attended, Sarah and Peter would've sat with Francis and his children waiting for the Examination to start. A bit after 10 a.m., Rebecca walked from Ingersoll's to the Meeting House and was escorted inside to begin her examination. John Hathorne questioned her, and Samuel Parris recorded the Examination.

Hathorne asked one of the afflicted, "What do you say, have you seen this Woman hurt you?"

One of them replied, "Yes, she beat me this morning,"

"Abigail, have you been hurt by this Woman?"

"Yes"

As Hathorne questioned Rebecca, Ann Putnam Jr cried out in the midst of a fit, that Goody Nurse was hurting her.

"Goody Nurse, here are two Ann Putnam Jr, the child, and Abigail Williams complaints of your hurting them; what do you say to it?"

Rebecca replied, "I can say before my eternal Father I am innocent, and God will clear my innocency,"

"Here is never a one in the Assembly who desires it, but if you are guilty, pray God to discover you," replied Hathorne.

Henry Kenny rose from the audience, hoping to speak.

"Goodman Kenny, what do you say?" inquired Hathorne

Henry entered a complaint saying that since Rebecca Nurse came into the Meeting House, he was seized twice with an "amazed condition."

Hathorne then said to Rebecca, "Here are not only these but here is the wife of Mr. Thomas Putman who accuses you by credible information and that both of tempting her to iniquity and of greatly hurting her."

"I am innocent and clear and have not been able to get out of doors these eight or nine days," replied Rebecca.

"Mr Edward Putman, give in what you have to say?" asked Hathorne

Edward Putnam then rose and gave evidence against Rebecca, [which was not recorded].

Hathorne asked Rebecca, "Is this true, Goody Nurse?"

She responded with, "I never afflicted any child, never in my life,"

"You see these accuse you, is it true?"

"No," affirmed Rebecca.

"Are you an innocent person related to this Witchcraft?"

Ann Putnam, Sr cried, "Did you not bring the Black man with you? Did you not bid me tempt God and die? How often have you eaten and drunk your domain?"

"What do you say to them?" asked Hathorne to Rebecca.

"Oh Lord help me," stated Rebecca, spreading her arms, and the afflicted were grievously vexed.

"Do you not see what a solemn condition these are in? When your hands are loose, the persons are afflicted."

Mary Walcott, aged 18, then deposed that while she had seen her before but here in this very moment Goody Nurse's specter was attacking her. Elizabeth Hubbard also confirmed a similar statement.

"Here are these two grown persons now accuse you; what say you? Do not you see these afflicted persons and hear them accuse you,"

"The Lord knows I have not hurt them; I am an innocent person,"

"It is very awful to all to see these agonies and you, an old Professor thus charged with contracting with the Devil by the effects of it, and yet to see you stand with dry eyes when there are so many whets,"

"You do not know my heart,"

"You would do well if you are guilty to confess & give Glory to God,"

"I am as clear as the child unborn."

"What uncertainty there may be in apparitions I know not, yet this with me strikes hard upon you that you are at this very present charged with familiar spirits;

this is your bodily person they speak to, they say now they see these familiar spirits come to your bodily person, now what do you say to that?"

"I have none, Sir,"

"If you have confessed and give glory to God, I pray God clears you if you are innocent, & if you are guilty, discover you. And therefore, give me an upright answer: have you any familiarity with these spirits?"

"No, I have none but with God alone,"

"How came you sick, for there is an odd discourse of that in the mouths of many?"

"I am sick to my stomach,"

"Have you no wounds?"

"I have none but old age,"

"You do know whether you are guilty, & have familiarity with the Devil, & now when you are here present to see such a thing as these testify a black man whispering in your ear, & birds about you what do you say to it?"

"It is all false. I am clear,"

"Possibly, you may apprehend you are no witch, but have you not been led aside by temptations that way?"

"I have not,"

"What a sad thing it is that a church member here & now and another of Salem should be thus accused and charged,"

A woman in her forties, Bathsheba Pope, cried out that Goody Nurse's specter was hurting her, knocking Pope off her seat.

"Tell us, have you not had visible appearances more than what is common in nature?"

"I have not nor ever had in my life,"

"Do you think these suffer voluntarily or involuntarily?"

"I cannot tell,"

"That is strange. One can judge."

"I must be silent,"

"They accuse you of hurting them, and if you think it is not unwillingly but by design, you must look upon them as murderers,"

"I cannot tell you what to think of it,"

Rebecca had a hard time understanding what Hathorne was asking her stating that "I did not think so," simply because she could not understand right what was said.

"Well, then, give an answer now. Do you think these suffer against their wills or not?"

"I do not think these suffer against their wills,"

"Why did you never visit these afflicted persons?"

"Because I was afraid I would have fits too,"

It was noted that upon the motion of her body the afflicted had fits followed upon the complainants abundantly and very frequently.

"Is it not an unaccountable case that when you are examined, these persons are afflicted?" stated Hathorne.

"I have got nobody to look to but God,"

Rebecca stirred her hands, the afflicted persons were seized with violent fits of torture.

"Do you believe these afflicted persons are bewitched?"

"I do think they are,"

"When this Witchcraft came upon the stage, there was no suspicion of Tituba.

She professed much love to that child Betty Paris, but it was her apparition that made the mischief, & why should not you also be guilty, for your apparition doth hurt also,"

"Would you have me belie myself,"

Rebecca held her neck on one side, and accordingly so were the afflicted taken, then Authority requiring it Samuel Parris read what he had in characters taken from Mr. Thomas Putnam's wife in her fits.

"What do you think of this?"

"I cannot help it; the Devil may appear in my shape,"

From this, her examination ends; Rebecca's remark of the Devil appearing in her shape went against the common belief that the Devil needed consent to appear in someone's shape. This common belief helped fan the flames of the witch hunt—causing the Witch Accusations to spread as it did, leading to the acceptance of spectral evidence in the courts and being the primary evidence against the accused. It's not the first time spectral evidence was used in a court case in the colonies or England. In 1662, at the Bury St. Edmunds witch trial, spectral evidence was the primary evidence against the elderly Amy Denny and Rose

Cullender. Judge Matthew Hale (no relation to the Reverend John Hale) allowed spectral evidence to be submitted. It set the precedent and made it acceptable in the future.

    Dorothy Good was examined after Rebecca, the young girl, confessed at her Examination and was committed to the Salem Jail alongside Rebecca, albeit inside the Jail Keeper's home. The Salem Jail was only eight years old, thirteen feet by twenty feet, but it wasn't a place in elite condition; a basement, two floors, surrounded by a palisade creating a yard for the prisoners to walk around. They were built only as temporary incarceration, with those waiting to be transferred to the Boston Jail for trial. The North River was barely a tenth of a mile from its gate; occasionally, the water would flood the dungeon of the jail. Seagulls squealed and perched on the palisades. A set of wooden stairs led to the second floor for the jailer's lodging; lesser "prisoners" would be kept on the first floor, unlike those who committed the capital crime of Witchcraft, who were held in the basement "dungeon."

    Behind the heavy studded wooden door was the open common space for the prisoners, the floors strewn with straw soaking up the urine and feces from its inhabitants. Light barely filled the room; its small windows were barred, keeping light and free-flowing air out. Chains were fixated on the walls so they could not move far once cuffed, stuck in the small, dank space. This accusation and the now incarceration of Rebecca angered her family further; perhaps news quickly spread to Topsfield, informing Mary what was happening to her sister. We can confirm that Sarah was infuriated at her sisters' accusation and the anger that exploded on Sacrament Sunday.

      On Sunday, March 28, the Meeting House in Salem Village began to fill with its members, ready for the service and its Communion to be held afterward for its covenant members. Sarah sat on her side of the Meeting House with the other women, likely hearing the whispers and gossip because of her sister's accusation. She looked forward, the spot where Rebecca once sat, now she sat in the Jail, a miserable place. She opened her small Bible, ready to follow along with the Minister's service; hoping he would calm the congregation.

Sarah and the congregation looked forward as the Minister entered the western door of the Meeting House.

He climbed the oak podium and opened his large copy of the Bible, and his voice bounced off the (what is that thing) and echoed into the ears of the congregation. Reading from the Book of John, Chapter 6, verse 70, "*Jesus answered them, Have not I chosen you twelve, and one of you is a devil?*" Sarah knew his motivation behind this, and she knew this story by heart about the betrayal of Christ by Judas. He was comparing her sister, a covenant member of the Church for twenty years, to a man like Judas. The Minister read on, but Sarah could not take it anymore; she rose from her box pew, opened the small door, and stood in the aisle before the Minister.

Their eyes locked; they both knew. Sarah turned her back to the Minster and caught a glimpse of her husband, Peter. Sarah opened the door and walked out, with the door making a loud clash as it slammed against the frame. As Sarah walked home, the service continued, and Mary Sibley was questioned because of her role in the witchcake. The congregation accepted her apology and took Communion. Peter still located in the church service likely looked around him as the other members uncomfortably watched on.

As one would predict, "Goody Cloyse" was soon on the lips of Abigail Williams and the others afflicted within the Village. It was only a matter of time for such a thing to happen.

Chapter 7
VÊ, VÊ, VÊ, Witchcraft

April 1692

Sarah had stormed from the Meeting House on Sabbath Day, and on March 31st, a day declared as a public fast to pray for the afflicted. Abigail Williams awoke during the night to see forty witches inside the Parsonage, mocking the fast and indulging in gluttony. Lit by the flames of the hearth, the specters of Sarah Cloyse and Sarah Good served blood and flesh to the participants. But the real Sarah Cloyse slept in her home; she likely knew what was to come; her sister Rebecca had been in jail only a few weeks by the beginning of April. Beginning on April 4th, a specter began to attack Abigail Williams, and the specter was that of Elizabeth Proctor. Abigail claimed that Proctor's specter pinched her, and then again, on the 6th, she once again returned and continued to pinch her and sit on her chest.

On April 4th, Captain Johnathan Walcott and Lieutenant Nathaniel Ingersoll had enough. They went into Salem Town to file an official complaint against Elizabeth Proctor and Sarah Cloyse. They were accused of afflicting Abigail Williams, John Indian, Mary Walcott, Ann Putnam Jr, and Mercy Lewis. The Magistrates John Hathorne and Johnathan Corwin decided they needed consultation from Boston to further the matter. So, they decided to wait for the Governor's Council of Assistants before issuing the arrest warrants. In the meantime, the specters of Cloyce and Proctor continued to plague the afflicted during that time. Abigail Williams claimed that both Elizabeth Proctor and her husband, John, afflicted her that same night.

    It wasn't until April 8th that Hathorne and Corwin received a reply that the Council would attend the next witchcraft hearing, and they issued the warrants. But, even before their arrest, the afflicted claimed that Sarah's specter was attacking them on the Sabbath Day. John Indian claimed that Sarah's specter drew blood after biting and pinching him. After hearing Sarah's name, Ephraim Sheldon saw Mercy Lewis fall into a seizure at Ingersoll's Ordinary. However, Ephriam asked Mercy whether Sarah's specter was the one that attacked her at that moment, to which Mercy replied, "No." Other bystanders asked whether it was "Goody Nurse" or "Goody Corey" and again if it was "Goody Cloyse." All to which Mercy Lewis replied no; Abigail Williams disagreed, claiming she *did* see the specters of Rebecca Nurse, Martha Corey, Sarah Cloyse, and Sarah Good. She even saw the specter of a bright, shining angel that scared away the specters of the witches.

Warrant for the Apprehension of Elizabeth Proctor and Sarah Cloyse, and Officer's Return

~~~

Salem April. 4'th 1692
There Being Complaint this day made (Before us) by Capt Jonat Walcott, and Lt Nathaniell Ingersoll both of Salem Village, in Behalf of their Majesties for themselves and also for several of their Neighbours Made Compl. Against Sarah Cloyse, the wife of Peter Cloyse of Salem Village, and Elizabeth Proctor, the wife of John Proctor of Salem Farms, for high Suspicion of

Sundry acts of Witchcraft donne or Committed by them upon the bodies of Abigail Williams, and John Indian both of Mr Sam Parris his family of Salem Village and Mary Walcott daughter of one of the above said Complainants And Ann Putnam and Mercy Lewis of the family of Thomas Putnam of Salem Village whereby great hurt and damage hath beene donne to the Bodys of s'd persons above named therefore Craved Justice.

You are, therefore, in their Majesty's names, hereby required to apprehend and bring before us Sarah Cloyse, the wife of Peter Cloyse of Salem Village, and Elizabeth Proctor, the wife of John Procter of Salem farmers, on Monday Morning Next being the Eleventh day of this Instant April about Eleven of the Clock, at the public Meeting house in the Towne, in order to their Examination Relating to the premises aboves'd and here of you are. Not to fail
Dated Salem Aprill 8'th 1692
*To George Herrick Marshall *John Hathorne*

of the County of Essex *Jonathan. Corwin Assists
You are likewise to warn & order Summon Eliz. Hubbard and Mary Warren not to faile of being present at the above s'd time & place to give in w't Evidence thay know therein
April. 11'th 1692, I have taken the persons of Sarah Cloyse and Elizabeth Proctor and brought them before this honorable Courte to answer above. I have also warned the above-named Elizabeth Hubbart as above per to answer as above
pr *Geo. Herrick Marshall of Essex

~~~

On Monday, April 11th, Sarah and Elizabeth were arrested from their homes, their young children watching as their mothers' were taken. No description of their arrest exists, but the officers return on their warrant. Passing by the Salem Village Meeting House, where Rebecca and the others were examined, the entourage continued onto Salem Town. To present this case before the members of the Governor's

Council. The two women were brought to the Salem Town Meeting House, where they were to be examined. The somewhat neglected Salem Town Meeting House was filled with a great assembly.

    They likely held the examinations in the Town due to the convenience of having members of the Governor's Council, including Thomas Danforth, the Deputy Governor, James Russell, Major Sam Appleton, Captain Samuel Sewall, and Issac Addington. John Hathorne, Jonathan Corwin, Samuel Parris, and the accusers of Elizabeth Proctor and Sarah Cloyse were also in attendance. Familiar with the building, Sarah and Elizabeth arrived at the two-story Meeting House, a rather large building that fell into disrepair in 1692. At sixty feet long, fifty feet wide, and twenty feet high. It was adorned with galleys and pews on the interior and stairs leading to said galleys with a bell on the roof; the windows were filled with four hundred and twenty-four square feet of glass, doors in the east, west, and south entrances.

    The proceedings began with the Magistrates (presumably Hathorne) inquiring about John Indian's afflictions, asking, "John, who hurt you?"

"Goody Proctor first, then Goody Cloyse," replied John.

"What did she do to you?" inquired Hathorne.

"She brought a book to me," stated John.

"John! Tell the truth, who hurts you? Have you been hurt?" bellowed Hathorne, likely wanting to show his strength before the Council.

"The first was a gentlewoman I saw," stated John.

"Who next?" asked Hathorne.

John replied, "Goody Cloyse,"

"But who hurt you next?" questioned Hathorne.

"Goody Proctor," stated John, confirming the presence of the other accused.

"What did she do to you?" asked Hathorne.

"She choked me, and brought the book," described John.

"How often did she come to torment you?" asked Hathorne

"A good many times, she and Goody Cloyse," confirmed John.

"Do they come to you in the night as well as the day?" inquired Hathorne.

"They come most in the day," stated John.

"Who?" wondered Hathorne.

"Goody Cloyse and Goody Proctor," affirmed John.

"Where did she take hold of you?" inquired Hathorne.

"Upon my throat, to stop my breath," described John, putting his own hands around his neck to show what was done to him.

"Do you know Goody Cloyse and Goody Proctor?" asked Hathorne.

"Yes, here is Goody Cloyse," turning and pointing to Sarah standing near him.

Sarah looked at John and asked him, "When did I hurt thee?"

"A great many times!" replied John, looking back at Sarah.

Angered by the man, Sarah shouted, "Oh, you are a grievous liar!"

The Magistrate continues his line of questioning towards John Indian, confirming whether it was Goody Cloyse who afflicted him. Of course, he responded yes, confirming she attacked him the previous day during the Sunday Meeting, causing blood to be drawn supposedly. Hathorne then turns his line of questioning towards Mary Walcott, asking her who hurt her. Mary mostly gives testimony against Sarah Cloyse, reiterating what John said previously about her specter coming to her to sign the book and attacking her. She fell into a fit, where a guard lifted Mary and brought her to Sarah; after, the fits ceased. After recovering, Mary Walcott added that sometimes Sarah's specter was in the company of her sister Rebecca Nurse and Martha Corey's specters on occasion. She soon fell into a fit in the room before them after giving her deposition against Sarah.

    Next was Abigail Williams. Hathorne asked her about the "Mock Sacrament" held inside the Salem Village Parsonage by the various forty specters of Witches. Abigail described seeing Sarah Cloyse and Sarah Good as the deacons serving blood and flesh, claiming they had it twice that day. The questioning returned to Mary Walcott, who seemed to have temporarily recovered from her afflictions.

Mary asked about the white specter that came to her at "Deacon (Nathaniel) Ingersoll's home." Mary described him as "*A fine grave man, and when he came, he made all the witches tremble.*" Abigail Williams joined in, confirming she, too, saw this "Fine man" who made the witches tremble. She added that the specters of Sarah Cloyse, Rebecca Nurse, Martha Corey, and Sarah Good were attacking them and later "*trembled.*"

    No matter what Sarah did or said, the accusers pointed out the spectral yellow birds that swarmed the Meeting House. Or how the "*Black Man*" whispered into Sarah's ear whenever she spoke, whenever her accusers fell into fits, they made Sarah reach out and touch them to allow the "diabolical fluid" pass back into her to make the fits cease. Sarah merely asked someone for a cup of water before fainting in the room. Likely, the heat of the packed Meeting House and the exhaustion of her day caused her to pass out. Upon seeing the sight of her fainting, many of the afflicted girls seized and fell into fits as well. One of them even exclaimed, "*Oh! Her spirit is gone to prison to her sister, Nurse!*"

Next was Elizabeth Proctor.

"Elizabeth Proctor! You understand where you are charged to be guilty of sundry acts of Witchcraft; what say you to it? Speak the truth, and so you that are afflicted must speak the truth, as you will answer it before God another day. Mary Walcott! Doth this woman hurt you?" asked Hathorne.

Surprisingly, Mary Walcott responded, "I never saw her as to be hurt by her,"

Hathorne then asked Mercy Lewis and Abigail Williams, but both couldn't respond, acting as if their mouths were being shut forcibly.

Attention then turned to John Indian, who responded by saying, "This is the woman that came in her shift and choked me,"

Hathorne then asked, "Did she ever bring the book?"

To which John answered, "Yes, Sir,"

"What to do?"

"To write (his name),"

"Are you sure of it?" asked Hathorne.

"Yes, Sir," affirmed John Indian.

Elizabeth's husband, John, who was watching from the audience, remarked how if he had John Indian in his custody, he'd beat the Devil out of him. Attention was then turned to Abigail Williams and Ann Putnam Jr, still held silent by an invisible specter. Finally, they asked Elizabeth Proctor, "What do you say, Goody Proctor, to these things?"

"I take God in Heaven to be my witness, that I know nothing of it, no more than the child unborn," replied Elizabeth.

Hathorne then asked Ann Putnam Jr if Elizabeth was the one doing this to her, to which Ann replied "Yes," and then fell into a fit at the sight of Proctor. Abigail Williams was then asked if Proctor's specter asked her to sign the Devil's book. Abigail confirmed this, claiming that the specter promised to ensure "she'd be well." They continued discussing if anyone else was in the book when Elizabeth told Abigail, "Dear child, it's not so. There is another judgment, dear child," Abigail and Ann soon fell into fits; they claimed that Elizabeth's specter was sitting on the beam of the Meeting House. Then, Elizabeth's husband, John, was accused; they claimed that his specter was there too and that he was a Wizard. Ann Putnam claimed that Elizabeth and John's specters attacked her then, and the whole Meeting House flew into chaos. Being in the Meeting House, John knew he was done at this very moment.

    Abigail Williams claims that she saw John's specter attack Goodwife Bathsheba Pope, causing her to fall and her feet to fly up into the air, which the real Mrs Pope did. The court asked John Proctor what he had said about these charges, to which he replied, "I know not, I am innocent." One of the Magistrates then remarked, "You see, the Devil will deceive you; the children could see what you were going to do before the woman was hurt. I would advise you to repentance, for the Devil is bringing you out." Abigail then saw the specter of Goodman Proctor attacking Sarah Bibber, which made Sarah Bibber, Mary Walcott, and the other girls all fall into fits.

    At some point during the Examination, Ann Putnam and Abigail Williams raised their fists to strike Elizabeth Proctor. But, at the moment their fingers outstretched and grazed Proctor's hood (a simple accessory worn over their coif, sometimes made of wool, silk, or linen), they fell into fits, claiming their fingers burned. The hearing ended, and the three were immediately put into the nearby Salem Jail, where she joined her sister Rebecca. That night, after the hearings, Edward Bishop Jr of Salem Village saw John Indian, deciding to take it upon himself to stop John's afflictions leaving him bloody. A few streets over, Sarah spent only the night here before she, Rebecca, John and Elizabeth Proctor, Dorothy Good, and Martha Corey were loaded into a cart to be sent to the Boston Jail the next day.

    The prisoners were followed by Martha's husband, Giles, and possibly Rebecca's son, Samuel, and Sarah's husband, Peter. The journey took most of the day, passing through swampy marshes and billowing fields. The sun beat down on the group, John, with his wife Elizabeth, not knowing that she was carrying a child that would save her life. Sarah, with her sister Rebecca, one could surmise the two women sang Psalms and prayed together, hoping that God may help them. Then, there was Martha Corey, likely still angrily gazing at her husband, who gave a deposition against her. But that would not matter as Giles would join her within a month and be accused of Witchcraft.

    The prisoners passed people on the road to Boston, and other travelers stopped to see who the prisoners were. Perhaps the onlookers thought they were merely lowly criminals, not witches. But, before the day was out, they had arrived at the Winnisimmet Ferry in present-day Chelsea, vastly different than the present-day site. Sarah and the other prisoners were loaded onto the ferry in a vast bay surrounding the peninsula of Boston. Giles and the other family members remained behind as the prisoners rowed across the bay.

    They approached the Shawmut Peninsula, which they knew as Boston, and the prisoners were disembarked in the North End section of Boston. The site was located on present-day Commercial Street; they were once again loaded into the cart and paraded through the crowded streets. The smells of the sea, fish, and the odor of the dirty city filled their noses, and the people living in the busy seaport noticed the prisoner cart. Some likely knew what was happening in Salem; word would've spread quickly of the newly suspected "witches" arriving in the city.

They passed the open pastures heading down the Street to the Mill Bridge, passing the tightly packed homes.

Mill Cove and Boston Harbor could easily be seen through the homes on the street. They passed over Mill Creek, the home of Thomas Brattle, which could be seen not far in the distance. They finally arrived at the intersection with Sudbury Street and took a left onto Prison Lane. The jail stood three stories high, built of stone and wood, its outer stone walls three feet thick. The doors were covered with iron spikes, "*the passageways like the dark valley of the shadow of death.*"

Like the Salem Jail, the Boston Jail was surrounded by a stone palisade where the prisoners could wander around. Inside the jail, a large common room on the first floor was bordered by the cells in which the prisoners slept. The prisoners joined Tituba, Sarah Good, and Sarah Osbourne, who had been there since the beginning of March. Along with dozens of other prisoners, including twenty-eight-year-old Elizabeth Emerson, who had been imprisoned on charges of murdering and concealing the deaths of her infant twins. The laws of the 17th-century forbade the concealment of the death of a "bastard" infant.

Not long after Sarah and Rebecca arrived at the Boston Jail, the eight-week-old daughter of John and Hannah Putnam died. In a later deposition, John and Hannah described the young baby having fits for two days prior. The young baby's fits would last up to five hours, crying senselessly, then they ceased, and the baby was dead. Infant mortality was common in colonial Massachusetts, but as with most things during the spring of 1692, they believed something more sinister was behind it.

Chapter 8
The Midnight Ride
April 21st, 1692

Warrant for the Apprehension of William Hobbs, Deliverance Hobbs, Nehemiah Abbot Jr, Sarah Wildes, Edward Bishop Jr., Sarah Bishop, Mary Black, and Mary English

There being a complaint made before us by Thomas Putnam and John Buxton of Salem Village yeomen, on behalf of themselves of their Majesties and for themselves and also for several of their neighbors. Against William Hobbs, husbandman and Deliverance his wife; Nehemiah Abbott Jr, weaver; Mary Esty, wife of Isaac Esty; Sarah Wildes, wife of John Wildes all of the Town of Topsfield or Ipswich. Edward Bishop husbandman and Sarah his wife of Salem Village; Mary Black a Negro of Lt. Nathaniel Putnam of Salem Village; also and Mary English the wife of Phillip English, Merchant in Salem for high *suspicion of sundry acts of Witchcraft done of committed by them lately on the bodies of Ann Putnam Jr and Mercy Lewis belonging to the family of the above said Thomas Putnam complainant and Mary Walcott the daughter of Capt. Johnathan Walcott of Salem Village and others. Whereby great hurt and damage hath been done to the bodies of said persons above named therefore crave justice.*

You are therefor required in their Majesties name hereby required to apprehend and bring William Hobbs, husbandman and his wife; Nehemiah Abbott Jr, weaver; Mary Esty, wife of Isaac Esty and all the rest above named tomorrow about ten of the forenoon at the house of Lt. Nathaniel Ingersoll in Salem Village. In order to their examination relating to the premises above said and hereof you are not to fail.

Dated Salem April 21'th 1692
John Hathorne
Jonathan Corwin

~~~

April 1692

A new specter had begun to afflict Anne Putnam Jr, Mercy Lewis, and Mary Walcott. Thomas Putnam, father of the afflicted Ann Putnam Jr and her afflicted mother, Ann Putnam Sr, filed a complaint against William and Deliverance Hobbs; Nehemiah Abbot Jr; Sarah Wildes; Mary Esty, all of Topsfield; Edward Jr and Sarah Bishop; Mary Black, slave of Nathaniel Putnam; and Mary English.

The next day, on the 22nd, the warrants were issued, and Ephraim Wildes and Marshall George Herrick split the arrests. When arresting Mary Esty, the Constable traveled up the Ipswich Road that passed through Esty and Towne's land, arriving at the small home of Mary and her family. Mary, being the woman she was, didn't resist and went with the Constable, who proceeded to arrest the others on the warrant. They traveled south, passing through the farms of the different families along the way; traveling over Mile Brook, they intersected with the other portion of Ipswich Road.

It is possible once Mary was loaded into the cart, her husband and eldest son hopped on their horses to follow. They turned right, passing onto the Meeting House Road, smaller than the main Ipswich Road. But it brought them through the center of Salem Village, passing the Meeting House and the home of the Sibley's. They passed the Meeting House, where the first examinations were held in the village, and soon they arrived at the home of Lt. Nathaniel Ingersoll, where Rebecca was held before her examination. Mary's wrists would've been kept bound preparing for her examination and beginning at ten o'clock; the prisoners were escorted downstairs for their examination.

The order is lost to history, but at some point, Mary was escorted to the barroom, where her examination began. As with Sarah's examination eleven days prior, the questioner was presumably Hathorne, with Samuel Parris transcribing.

When Mary entered the room, the afflicted fell into their fits. Hathorne asked, "Does this woman hurt you?"

Several of their mouths were stopped, and others fell into fits. Abigail Williams confirmed it was "Goody Esty," with Mary Walcott and Ann Putnam Jr.

confirming. John Indian was present, healing from his bruises sustained by Edward Bishop, stating he saw her specter with the specter of Deliverance Hobbs.

Hathorne asked Mary, "What do you say? Are you guilty?"

"I can say before Christ Jesus I am free," replied Mary.

"You see these accuse you," pointed out Hathorne.

"There is a God," stated Mary.

Hathorne asked the afflicted, "Has she brought the book to you?"

The afflicted couldn't speak; Hathorne asked Mary, "What have you done to these children?"

"I know nothing," she affirmed.

"How can you say you know nothing when you see these tormented and accuse you that you know nothing?" asked Hathorne.

"Would you have me accuse myself?" replied Mary.

"Yes, if you be guilty, how far have you complied with Satan whereby he takes advantage against you?"

Ever respectful, Mary responded, "Sir, I never complied but prayed against him all my days; I have no compliance with Satan in this. What would you have me do?"

"Confess if you be guilty," stated Hathorne.

"I will say it, if it was my last time, I am clear of this sin," confirmed Mary.

"Of what sin?" asked Hathorne.

"Of witchcraft," stated Mary.

Hathorne once again asked the afflicted, "Are you certain this is the woman?"

Once again, the afflicted couldn't speak but only convulsed, but soon, Ann Putnam Jr. stated that this was the woman and that her specter said Mary's name. Hathorne turned to Mary once again and asked, "It's marvelous to me that you should sometimes think they are bewitched, and sometimes not several confess that they have been guilty of bewitching them."

"Well, Sir, would you have me confess that I never knew?" replied Mary.

Mary clenched her hands together, causing Mercy Lewis's hands to clench together. Hathorne pointed out, "Look now, your hands are open; her hands are open!"

Hathorne asked the afflicted, "Is this the woman?"

The afflicted made signs but could not speak until Ann Putnam Jr and Elizabeth Hubbard cried out, "Oh! Goody Esty, Goody Esty, you are the woman, you are the woman!" Mary bowed her head, causing the afflicted's necks to bow as well; Hathorne demanded, "Put up her head, for while her head is bowed, the necks of these are broken,"

A guard righted Mary's head, and Hathorne asked her, "What do you say to this?"

"Why God will know," replied Mary.

"Nay God knows know," stated Hathorne.

"I know he does," responded Mary.

"What did you think of the actions of others before your sisters came out? Did you think it was witchcraft?" asked Hathorne.

"I cannot tell," replied Mary.

"Why do you not think it's witchcraft?" questioned Hathorne.

"It is an evil spirit, but whether it be witchcraft, I do not know," stated Mary.

At the end of the examination, several of the afflicted confirmed her specter brought the book to them, and they soon fell into fits. Mary was removed from the room, and the proceedings were continued for any other accused that remained that day. Depositions against Mary from Margaret Reddington and Samuel Smith were also heard that day. Goody Reddington deposed that her specter brought her a piece of meat last Thanksgiving. Samuel Smith stated that five years prior, Mary called him out for rude behavior and that a quarter of a mile from the Esty home, the stone wall rattled, and he received a blow on his shoulder.

After examination, the court ordered that Mary Esty, William Hobbs, Deliverance Hobbs, Edward and Sarah Bishop, Sarah Wildes, Mary Black, and Mary English were committed to the Salem Jail. Mary was kept there for the following month, while Sarah and Rebecca remained committed to the conditions of the Boston jail. It's known that the family Rebecca visited often, likely informing Sarah and Rebecca of Mary's accusation. The accusations spread quickly; after this batch of nine arrests, more would be arrested within weeks. As well as one of the most interesting tales of the Salem Witch Trials would unfold involving Mary Esty.

May 18th, 1692

Mary had been incarcerated in the Salem Jail for around a month; she remained in the Salem Jail while George Jacobs Sr, Giles Cory, William Hobbs, Edward and Sarah Bishop, Bridget Bishop, Sarah Wildes, Mary Black, Mary English, Alice Parker, and Ann Pudeator were sent to the Boston Jail. Likely as they were all to proceed ahead to trial. Deliverance and Abigail Hobbs, Mary Warren, Sarah Churchill, Margaret Jacobs, Abigail Soames, Rebecca Jacobs, Sarah Buckley, and Mary Whitridge were imprisoned alongside Mary. The court had begun to look at the evidence against her, reviewing the afflicted who had claimed her specter was attacking them.

Ann Putnam Jr and Mary Walcott could no longer confirm or deny whether Mary Esty was the one afflicting them. Elizabeth Hubbard likely joined Ann and Mary in the uncertainty, but Mercy Lewis remained adamant that Mary was her afflictor. The court, however, decided to release Mary; Nemiah Abott Jr was also released after his arrest due to similar circumstances. Mary returned home to

Topsfield, staying with her son Isaac Jr just down the road from her home. Having Mary at home with Isaac Jr was more manageable as the newly married, childless couple would allow them to take care of Mary while his father could tend to the farm.

    The family could breathe now that Mary was home, providing hope for the Nurse and Sarah's elder children from her first marriage. However, before the news of her release could be relayed to her sister in Boston, things would take a rapid turn for the worse. At some point on May 19th, Mercy Lewis was transferred to the home of John Putnam; here, she fell into afflictions once more. Her condition quickly deteriorated, and by the 20th, her afflictions worsened, and she was bedridden. Those around Mercy very quickly suspected who was doing this to the eighteen-year-old.

    Beginning around nine in the morning on May 20th, Hannah Putnam sent Samuel Abbey to retrieve her husband's young cousin, Ann Putnam Jr. They then retrieved Abigail Williams, perhaps in hopes both girls could confirm their suspicions. Along the way; the event was slowly becoming public. During the trip, both

Abigail and Ann claimed that they saw the specter of Mary Esty as they traveled down the road. They arrived at the home, seeing Mercy in a "*sad condition.*" both Abigail and Ann immediately claimed that they saw the specter of Mary Esty afflicting Mercy. They also saw and identified the specters of John Willard and Mary Witheridge choking Mercy in a "*dreadful manner.*"

According to the afflicted, the specters did not take long to turn their attention to themselves. Ann, Abigail, and the now present Mary Walcott fell into fits blinded by the specters, with Mary Walcott later testifying, "*Terrified me much and she told me that she had blinded all our eyes that ware affected only Mercy Lewis for she said that she had not power to do it on that day she was cleared,*" The specters tormented the girls by blinding them, and choking them with a chain. As the sun began to lower, it was informed to those who could not see or hear the specters that they had until midnight or else Goody Esty would kill Mercy.

By eight o'clock that night, John Putnam returned to the home where a large crowd had formed in the main room where

Mercy lay. Elizabeth Hubbard returned with him, where she was almost immediately attacked by the specters Mary Esty, John Willard, and Mary Witheridge. John Putnam and John Hutchinson made great haste to Salem Town to procure the warrant to arrest Mary Esty. Mercy Lewis would say, "Dear Lord, receive my soul, Lord let them not kill me quite. Pray for the salvation of my soul, for they will kill me,"

      Riding through the dark, they arrived in Salem Town. Thankfully, John Hathorne lived in the center of Town. They explained the situation and informed him how Mary's specter would kill Mercy Lewis if they did not arrest her before midnight. Somehow, the warrant for the second arrest of Mary Esty was drawn up, informing George Herrick to immediately ride to Topsfield to apprehend Mary.

~~~

Salem May 20th 1692
There is a complaint made before me on this day by John Putnam Jun'r. and Benjamin Hutchinson, both of Salem Village, for themselves and also for their Neighbours, in

behalf of their Majesties against Mary Esty, the wife of Isaac Esty of Topsfield, for sundry acts of witchcraft by her Committed yesterday and this present day of the date hereof upon the bodies of Ann Putnam, Mercy Lewis, Mary Walcott, and Abigail Williams of Salem Village to the wrong and Injury of their body, therefore, crave Justice.
*John Putnam Junior
*Benjamin Hutchinson
To the Marshall of the County of Essex or dept or Constables of Salem You are in their Majest's names hereby required to apprehend and forthwith bring before me at the house of Mr. Thomas Beadles in Salem the Body of Mary Esty the wife Isaac Esty of Topsfield to be Examined Relating to sundry acts of witchcraft by her Committed yesterday and this present day according to Complaint aboves'd and hereof you are not to faile Dated Salem
May 20th 1692
*John: Hathorne. Assist
per order of the Councill.

*I have taken the body of the above-named Mary Esty and brought her at the time and place above-named
Per me *Geo: Herrick
Marshall of Essex*

~~~

    The Esty family likely suspected something of this nature; hearing the cart coming up the road, Isaac Jr hid his Mother in the root cellar of his home. Mary huddled in the darkness, the tiny slivers of light peering through the cracks in the wooden floor from the hearth. The suspicious quiet was broken by the loud raps of Herrick's fist on the home door. Isaac opened it and asked why they were present at his home. Herrick responded by reading the warrant for her arrest.

    Isaac denied his mother's presence, but Herrick pushed forward, entering the home. Inspecting the room, there weren't many places for Mary to hide; she would've heard his leather boots hit against the floor. Coming closer and closer to the entrance to the cellar, Herrick opened the cellar door, not being a stupid man. Revealing Mary huddled beneath the floor, pulling her from the basement, he tied Mary's hands behind her back. Her son loudly argued his Mother's apprehension, and Mary agreed she would go with Herrick, knowing there was no reason to fight.

Mary was led out and placed in the cart, riding through the darkness of Topsfield and Salem Village. Arriving at the home of Thomas Beadle, who ran a tavern in Salem Town, likely prepared for Mary's arrival. She remained upstairs pending her second examination, which was lost to history. But, satisfied with his actions, Herrick returned to Mercy Lewis and informed him that her affliction had been apprehended. When he arrived at the home of John Putnam, Mercy was in a violent seizure, stopping and responding to this by saying, "I had rather go into the winding sheet than set my hand to the book," Her condition worsened and was up until daybreak, and eventually, she recovered.

From this event, the afflicted named four more people: Sarah Proctor, daughter of Elizabeth and John Proctor; Sarah Bassett, sister-in-law of Elizabeth Proctor; Mary DeRich, sister of Elizabeth Proctor; and

Susannah Roots, a poor widow from Beverly. By the 23rd, all of the men and women accused during this escapade would be incarcerated in the Boston Jail, with someone even accused during the examinations held on the 23rd. Mary joined her sisters, who had been there for over a month, and the three sisters were together. Waiting for an inevitable fate.

Part 3:
May 1692-September 1711

Chapter 9
Hear and Determine

May 23rd, 1692

Leaving the Village on a dry, hot, and windy day made the journey to Boston uncomfortable. Mary Esty had spent her weekend being examined by the Magistrates in Salem Town and later the Village. Made to participate in a touch test, Elizabeth Cary of Charlestown, who came to watch as a spectator, ended up among the accused. One of the afflicted accused Mary's specter of stabbing them with a spindle; said spindle was discovered missing from one of the homes in the village. Mercy Lewis later produced said spindle, claiming that she fought Mary's specter and stole it.

Mary Esty, Abigail Soames, Susannah Roots, Sarah Bassett, Mary DeRich, Benjamin Proctor, and Elizabeth Cary arrived in Boston later that day. Traveling through the fields over the harbor and down the road that led them to the Boston Jail, adding to the dozens of accused already in there. One could only imagine the shock Sarah and Rebecca felt at the sight of Mary in chains; her arrest, release, and re-arrest came all within seventy-two hours. The last Sarah and Rebecca knew, Mary was either imprisoned or released, but they likely got their sister's full story of the experience.

As the summer heat grew, the smell and condition of the jail worsened; one could only imagine the disgusting smells that reeked. Sarah Osbourne, of the original group accused, died on May 10th; her already poor health was worsened by the conditions of the jail; she was only forty-nine years old. The people in the Jail waited to hear what would come of their fates, and they all likely assumed the trials would happen in Boston. As with all previous Capital Cases, they were held in the Boston Town House, and most Witchcraft cases ended with an acquittal. Convictions were rare, and often, they were reprieved in the instances of Hugh Parsons 1651 and Elizabeth Morse 1679. In the case of Eunice Cole of Hampton, it was common for people to be put on Trial more than once; she was tried twice in 1656, found guilty and reprieved and again in 1673; she was arrested in 1680 but was let go.

The new Governor had only arrived on May 14th, amid the ongoing accusations, and on the 27th of that month, a Special Court of Oyer and Terminer was called to hear the cases. The Court consisted of Lt. Governor William Stoughton, Bartholomew Gedney, John Hathorne, Jonathan Corwin, Samuel Sewall, Waitstill Winthrop, John Richards, and Nathaniel Saltonstall to "hear and determine" the cases against the accused. On May 31st, Sarah and Mary said goodbye to her sister Rebecca as she, Bridget Bishop, The Proctors, Sarah Good, Susannah Martin, Alice Parker, John Willard, and Tituba were transported back to the Salem Jail.

June 1692

In the meantime, Rebecca's incarceration, her husband and family, with the help of Israel Porter, developed a petition in support of Rebecca.

"We whose names are hereunto subscribed being desired by Goodman Nurse to declare what we knew concerning his wives conversation for time past: we can testify to all whom it may concern that we have

known her for many years and according to our observation her life and conversation was according to her profession and we never had any cause or grounds to suspect her of any such thing as she is now accused of."

    Thirty-nine people had signed in support of Rebecca; many neighbors had relatives who accused Rebecca of Witchcraft. Namely, those related to the Putnams and Holten Families were divided in their thoughts about her accusations. Sarah Holten would give testimony against Rebecca regarding the suspiciously untimely death of her husband, Benjamin Holten. While Benjamin's parents signed the petition in support of Rebecca. Arriving back in Salem, depositions were beginning to be heard against her and other accused in a formal setting. An official summons was being sent out for witnesses of the supposed acts of witchcraft committed by her to appear at her Grand Jury hearing on the 3rd.

    Evidence is also piled against Sarah in this testimony against Rebecca. Ann Putnam Sr.'s deposition was among the first depositions heard against Sarah Cloyse.

Deposition of Ann Putnam Sr. v. Rebecca Nurse, Sarah Cloyce, Sarah Bishop, & Elizabeth Cary

"The deposition of Ann Putnam, the wife of Thomas Putnam, testified and said that on June 1st, 1692. the Apperishtion of Rebecca Nurse did again fall upon me and almost choak me. She told me that now she was come out of prison she had power to afflict me and that now she would afflict me all this day long and would kill me if she could for she told me she had killed Benjamin Holton and John Fuller and Rebecca Shepard. She also told me that she and her Sister Cloyse and Edward Bishop, wife of Salem Village, had killed young John Putnam's child because young Putnam had said that it was no wonder they were witches for their Mother was so before them and because they could not avenge themselves on him, they did kill his child. Immediately, they appeared to me, and six children in winding sheets called me Aunt, which did most grievously fright me. And they told me that they were my sister Baker's children of

Boston and that Goody Nurse and Mistress Cary of Charleston and an old deaf woman at Boston had murdered them. And charged me to go and tell these things to the magistrates or else they would tear me to pieces for their blood did cry for vengeance. also, they appeared to me, my own sister Bayley, and three of her children in winding sheets and told me that Goody Nurse had murdered them."
~Ann Putnam Sr on June 2nd, 1692

~~~

Ann Senior's statement, "Putnam had said that it was no wonder they were witches for their Mother was so before them," brings forward the rumor that Joanna Towne was accused of Witchcraft. No further documents survive mentioning an accusation against Joanna. Much to the surprise of many, the court proceedings were moved from Boston, where they were expected. To the Town of Salem, mostly for the convenience of the accusers and their families. The hearings would be heard on the second floor of the Town House located in the center of present-day Washington St. Built in the 1670s, using timbers from the old Meeting House, it had a Latin School on the first floor where the students would occasionally snoop on the court hearings held above.

 Slowly but surely, Sarah received word from her husband and her sister's family on her sister's status. Very soon, they learned that Rebecca would be going to Trial; her Grand Jury did not favor her, and she was indicted on four counts against Ann Putnam Jr, Mary Walcott, Elizabeth Hubbard, and Abigail Williams. Before her Grand Jury, Rebecca underwent two physical examinations, a process where they looked over Rebecca's body for signs of "witches' teats." Finding a "piece of flesh," that was deemed suspicious; her daughters testified that any strange marks that they found during her process were due to "An infirmity of the body for many years."

 Of the six depositions heard by the Grand Jury, four were against Rebecca, and two supported her. Rebecca was returned to the Salem Jail to await her fate; while the first of the trials began, Bridget (formerly Oliver), Bishop of Salem Town, Sarah's former neighbor, was tried and convicted on

June 2nd, 1692. William Stoughton signed Bridget's death warrant on June 8th, 1692, and her execution was scheduled for June 10th, 1692.

Sarah knew that with the quick trial and execution of Bridget, the same could happen to her or her sisters. And seeing the young daughter of Sarah Good accused, one could surmise Sarah's worry at her own children's accusation; her youngest was only seven. Rebecca's family and adult children visited her, Mary's husband, and Sarah's, respectively. One has to wonder if any of Sarah's children, at least her elder son Benjamin, who was twenty-seven at the time of his Mother's accusation, visited her alongside Peter.

On June 18th, Sarah was returned to the Salem Jail alongside her sister Mary Esty, George Burroughs, George Jacobs Sr, Giles and Martha Cory, Ann Pudeator, Sarah Wildes, Susannah Roots, and Dorcas Hoar. The move likely made Sarah anxious; by this time, seventy-two people were incarcerated, one executed, and two died in Jail. Sarah and Mary joined Rebecca in the much smaller and quickly cramped basement of the Salem Jail. One hopes the three sisters comforted one another in one of the most stressful moments in Rebecca's life.

Ten days after her sisters' arrival, Rebecca was removed from the Salem Jail, her trial was scheduled to begin. Rebecca was led from the jail, her health deteriorated, and she could barely walk; she was likely carried up the stairs to the second floor of the Town House, where she was tried. Rebecca was led to the docket, where she was made to stand as her trial proceeded; her accusers sat nearby, occasionally playing their usual games. The Magistrates sat in their black suits, reading the Depositions against her; two of them included testimony against Sarah herself.

~~~

Deposition of Sarah Stephens & Margery Pasque v. Rebecca Nurse, Sarah Cloyce, & Faith Black

"The Deposition of Sarah Stephens aged [?] & Margery Pasque aged [?] testify that the June 21st Last past being improved in the holding of Jemima Rea suddenly seized with strange fits, they heard the said Jemima in her fitts cry out much upon Goody Nurse,

Goody Cloyce & Goody Black, & said, What you cannot do it alone, & you brought this woman [to] help you: Why did you bring her? She was never complained of. Goody Cloyce (as these Deponents suppose) answered that the Devil would not suffer her any longer to be a Witch; she must be brought out. And the said Jemima complained that Goody Cloyce Pricks & Pinches her, and the said Jemima (as they understood by her discourse) was told by the said Cloyce that one Lord's day when she ran out of the meeting house from the Sacrament in a great rage, had her Master met her at the garrison gate just before the Fore-doer of the meeting house, to which Master she made a Courtesy, & at that time set her hand to his book & when she took her leave of him she made another Courtesy And farther these Deponents say that the said Jemima spake to this purpose in six or seven fits one after another, & that the said Cloyce had done, & bid these two deponents hold her hands that she might not so do; & also the said Jemima when recovered of her, fits confirmed what she had spoken in her fits these Deponents & further saith not."

Deposition of John Putnam Jr. & Hannah Putnam v. Rebecca Nurse, Mary Esty, & Sarah Cloyse

"*The Deposistion of John Putnam weaver: and Hannah his wife who testifieth and saith that our child which died about the middle of April 1692: was as well and as thriveing a child as most was: tell it was about eight weeks old: but awhile affter that I the said John Putnam had reported something which I had heard consarning the mother of Rebecca Nurse, Mary Esty, and Sarah Cloyse I myself was taken with strange kind of fit, but it pleased Almighty God to Deliver me from them, but quickly after this our poor young child was taken about midnight with strange and violent fits: which did most grievously affright us acting much like to the poor bewitched persons when we thought they would indeed have died: where upon we sent for our Mother Putnam in the night immediately: and as soon as she came and saw our child she told us that she feared there was an evell hand upon it: and also as fast as possibly could be we got a Doctor to it: but all he did give it could doe it no good: but it continued in strange and violent fits for about Two days and Two nights and then departed this life by a cruel and violent death being enough to pierce a stony hart for to the best of our understanding it was near five hours a dying"*

~~~

  Rebecca stood for hours as people came forth and testified against her, by the end of the Trial, nine people on top of the four from her grand jury spoke against Rebecca. However, ten people spoke in Rebecca's favor, including the two from her Grand Jury; the evidence was practically fifty-fifty. Bridget's Trial was cut and dry, but Rebecca's wasn't; neighbors spoke for and against her, and her family spoke for her. Eight of the ten depositions were regarding her accusers, Sarah Bibber, Elizabeth Hubbard, Mercy Lewis, Susannah Sheldon, and Abigail Williams. Sarah Nurse,

Rebecca's daughter-in-law, said that she saw Sarah Bibber pull the pins from her clothes and stick them beneath her fingernails. She then stated that Sarah cried out that Rebecca's specter had attacked her, sticking pins in her. The other testimony against Sarah Bibber stated she was "A woman of an unruly, turbulent spirit, and double-tongued."

After the evidence was heard and recorded, the jury deliberated and decided its verdict. Rebecca and her supporters held their breath, expecting the same verdict as Bridget earlier that month. They believed in God, hoping their prayers would be answered, that Rebecca would be cleared and that she could return home.

The jury returned with their verdict
"*Not Guilty*"

Rebecca's family and supporters cheered and were grateful, but the bliss would not last. Upon hearing the verdict, the afflicted fell into violent fits before the jury, and William Stoughton stated that he was not satisfied with the verdict. The Court had recessed, and during this, they went to look over the evidence to discuss the effects the verdict had on the afflicted. They were looking at the evidence and saw Rebecca's remark, which was somewhat confusing to Thomas Fiske. When Deliverance Hobbs was brought before the Court to testify against Rebecca, she remarked, "*What, do these persons give in evidence against me now? They used to come among us.*" A simple statement that Rebecca had made regarding Deliverance was "Of her company," meaning Deliverance was a fellow prisoner.

    The Court, however, did not know this, so Thomas asked Rebecca what she had meant by this statement. Unfortunately, Rebecca, who was seventy-one and hard of hearing, did not hear the question he asked. Then, attempting one more time to ask Rebecca what she had meant to no response, the jury reconvened and changed her verdict once more to "Guilty." Thomas Fiske later stated, "*But made no reply, nor interpretation of them. Whereupon these words were to me a principal Evidence against her.*" Rebecca was returned to the jail, where her family would soon join her, Sarah, and Mary in hopes of comforting her.

After Rebecca, Sarah Good, Susannah Martin, Elizabeth Howe, and Sarah Wildes were all tried and found guilty. Sarah and Mary remained by their sister's side as she attempted to tell the Court about the situation to no avail as someone wrote the statement for her. Then, on July 3rd, a fate worse than death in the eyes of the Puritan community, Rebecca was excommunicated. They were making the short distance from the Jail to the dilapidated Salem Town Meeting House before the Reverend Nicolas Noyes. Who had the congregation vote, and unanimously she was expelled from the physical Church and spiritually from her reserved place in heaven; soul, as they believed, damned to hell for all eternity.

On the 4th of July, one last ray of hope for Rebecca came; her new verdict and pending hanging did not sit well with many people. The evidence and petition was looked at once more, the thirty-nine signatures reminding the Court of the already messy opinion. Somehow, Rebecca's family persuaded Thomas Fisk to submit his statement about why the Court changed its verdict and the evidence behind it. Rebecca even had someone take a statement from her, signing it with her mark to be submitted. The paper was submitted to the Court in Boston; but the afflicted claimed they were tormented upon hearing of this.

    The sisters were huddled together, the long days and nights in the basement of the jail passing by as the dreaded day came closer. On July 12th, the warrant for the executions of Rebecca, Sarah Good, Elizabeth Howe, Susannah Martin, and Sarah Wildes was signed by William Stoughton. The reprieve was revoked, and an unknown gentleman from Salem had persuaded the Governor to rescind this appeal. The last hope was dashed for Rebecca and her family; her fate resigned to the Gallows, and her soul was damned to hell. July 19th would be the last day of Rebecca's life, with her sister beside her in her final week. One could only surmise the emotion felt by Sarah and her family at the thought of Rebecca's forthcoming execution. Rebecca's children came to visit their Mother one last time before they would never be able to again.

    The morning of July 19th came; it was hot and dry, and the smell of rain filled the noses of the people in the Jail. The guards entered the basement where the "*Witches*" were kept, arriving early at eight o'clock in the morning; the sounds of Rebecca's heavy chains clattered as the guards and his men lifted her up. Nothing more could be done to help Rebecca; her sisters tearfully watched as she was escorted from the basement cell, never seen again as the men led her to the cart. So, too, did they take Elizabeth How, Sarah Good, Sarah Wildes, and Susannah Martin, five women, to be hanged on this arid day. The cart left the Jail yard with the five women; a feeling of anguish could've been felt, one surmising the emotion at what would happen to her sister. It was only a matter of time until the next round of Trials occurred; would it be Sarah's turn?

Chapter 10
We Two Sisters

July 28th, 1692

By the end of the summer, accusations had spread widely throughout the county. The frontier towns of Andover, Haverhill, and Billerica began to have their own accused. Many towns had begun to "borrow" the afflicted; Elizabeth Ballard and Timothy Swan had fallen into a mysterious illness in Andover. The likes of which couldn't be explained, Joseph called for the afflicted of Salem Village to visit his wife in hopes of explaining her illness. Upon arriving, they claimed to have seen the specters of Mary Lacy Sr and her daughter, Mary Lacy Jr, attacking her. Warrants were issued, and the Andover portion of the Witch Panic began; during this, Sarah's former sister-in-law, Mary (Tyler) Bridges, would be arrested; Mary had wed Edmund's brother John in 1678.

Sarah and Mary had met the new batch of accused who were apprehended from Haverhill on the 28th, also charged with afflicting Elizabeth Ballard, who had died the previous day. Mary Green and Hannah Bromage of Haverhill were arrested for afflicting Timothy Swan, and during their examinations, Mary Bridges confessed and implicated them in attacking Swan and Ballard. The Magistrates deemed enough evidence for a trial, and Hannah Bromage was indicted for afflicting Mary Walcott. However, as the Salem Jail was quickly filling, the Court ordered that Sarah Cloyse, Mary Esty, Hannah Bromage, and Mary Green be placed in Irons and sent to the Ipswich Jail.

      The journey from the Salem Jail to the Ipswich Jail was not as terrible as the one to Boston, a few hours at most. Passing the hill where five people have been hanged on the outskirts of town likely made any of the accused nervous. Sarah and Mary could only imagine Rebecca's last moments on the Gallows, wondering if her soul was genuinely damned to hell regardless of her innocence. The cart bounced and rattled along the dirt road, passing by fields and forests along the way. In the occasional home with a tiny wisp of smoke leaving the chimney, the summer heat likely required many families to cook in the lean-to kitchen to make the heat more bearable.

    They arrived at the Ipswich Jail, roughly the same size as the Salem Jail, plus an extra floor. It was built in 1652 to accommodate the other prisoners in the colony, as the sole Jail in Boston could no longer contain all of its prisoners. Finished with daub on the interior and clapboards outside, it presented as any other small county jail. This jail, however, was known for breakouts, being the scene of the first jailbreak in the colony's history. Sarah, Mary, and the other accused were removed from the cart and ushered inside, their iron shackles remaining on their wrists.

    Among the fellow prisoners was Mistress Mary Bradbury, an elderly respected woman from Salisbury accused in late June 1692; Rachel Clenton of Ipswich, accused in late March 1692, one of the few to be charged outside of the outbreak; and Ann Pudeator from Salem Town, who was transferred here at an unknown date. Like the Salem and Boston Jails, the accused remained in the common room, likely on the first floor. Here, it's recorded that many prisoners were made to begin the laborious process of making flax and hemp cloth, and between working on making linen and hemp cloth, Sarah and Mary languished in the hot Jail.

August
  Being remanded here during the hot summer heat would've made anyone uncomfortable. Jail Fever was a common illness that killed many people incarcerated before measures were taken to improve jail conditions hundreds of years later. The weather would've worsened as July turned into August; occasional family visits were expected, however, lightening the mood. Peter often visited, likely bringing his and Sarah's children to see her and her aunt; he visited so often that Samuel Parris noted it in the Church Record Books. His absence from the Sacrament and that of Samuel Nurse and his wife were also noticed.
  On the 2nd and 23rd of August, Sarah watched as Mary Green broke out of jail with the assistance of her brother-in-law. On the first attempt, she was very quickly found and re-apprehended. The attempt was futile; the second attempt was almost successful. Mary was gone for a day and a

half, likely being hidden by family in nearby Rowley. But, by the 25th, Mary was returned to the Jail, perhaps with heavier irons than before to keep her locked away. Her sister, who is of the same name, was busy being transported to and from the Ipswich Jail during her grand jury hearing. Three statements were heard against her, most of the evidence coming from the show of her second arrest in May; she was officially indicted on two counts against Mercy Lewis and Elizabeth Hubbard.

  The courts in Salem were busy as well; the trials of Martha Carrier, John and Elizabeth Proctor, John Willars, George Jacobs Sr, and George Burroughs were beginning. All were found guilty, but Elizabeth was found pregnant, so they granted her a reprieve as a result. More accused were also arrested: Mary Clark on August 4th, Margaret Scott of Rowley, Elizabeth Johnson Jr on August 10th, Sarah and Thomas Carrier on August 10th, and Abigail Faulkner on August 11th, to name a few. The Jails filled quickly; most of those from Haverhill, Salisbury, Gloucester, Ipswich, and Rowley were incarcerated in Ipswich.

On August 19th, the next round of executions took place in Salem, drawing a large crowd as they happened. By noon, in the hot summer sun, Martha Carrier, John Proctor, George Burroughs, George Jacobs Sr, and John Willard were hanged. Cotton Mather, a Minister from Boston, arrived witnessing the hangings. Over the next month, the jails were filled with more and more people, and soon, opinions began to change against the trials. But an overwhelming majority still called for "justice" for the afflicted.

September

As the month changed and the weather began to cool, the Court of Oyer and Terminer sat again. On September 5th, the court-appointed midwives and surgeons physically examined Sarah Cloyce, Mary Esty, Rachel Clinton, Dorcas Hoar, Mary Bradbury, Martha, and Giles Corey. A process that looked at any "unnatural" part of the accused body could be used against them. The midwives did find a suspicious *"teat"* on the body of Mary Esty. Next, the official court summons was issued for witnesses against Sarah, her sister, Giles, and Martha Cory. The legal proceedings were beginning against Sarah; she knew it was only a matter of time before she found herself at the bar in the Salem Town House facing her grand jury or trial. From there, Sarah knew it would be only a foregone conclusion of her fate, joining the already eleven hanged and several deaths in Jail.

    The next day, another round of court summons was issued, and in this was named Sarah and Mary's sister-in-law Mary Towne and her children William, Samuel, Rebecca, and Elizabeth. They were likely ordered to appear to give testimony against their family; why they would be summoned is unsure. Perhaps since around this time, the afflicted were going to other towns such as Andover; they saw or believed the specters of Sarah and Mary to attack their own family somehow. However, Mary Towne, the resilient woman she was, decided to remain behind, as did her children named in the warrant.

    Sending her excuse to the Court, Mary wrote, or at least had someone write for her,

"*Right honored: the Constable of Topsfield had served a warrant on me and two of my sons and two of my daughters to appear this day at Salem. I humbly beg that your honors will not impute anything concerning our not coming as contempt of authority, for were I myself or any of my family sent for in any capacity of coming, we would come, but we are in a Strange condition. Most of us can scarcely get out of our beads we are so weal and not able to read at all. As for my daughter Rebecca she has strange fits sometimes she is knocked down all of a sudden, and that especially is her Aunt Esty be but named.*"

Whatever illness afflicted Rebecca was still deemed necessary; perhaps it was just a simple illness, but coincidence was not understood in the 17th Century. The excuse is rather convenient, at least in the eyes of the Court; Ephraim Wildes tapped on their door the next day. Mary begrudgingly left with her daughter Rebecca, and they arrived in Salem within a few hours. Whatever testimony was provided was not used for or against Mary Esty, but instead, Sarah was indicted for afflicting her niece. It's likely Sarah's accusers stated that Sarah's specter had made her niece ill to keep her away from the Court. It's unlikely Mary would allow Rebecca to give testimony that could put Sarah to death, but it's a mystery that has been lost to history.

    Since the delay of Mary Towne and Rebecca, the evidence against Mary Esty couldn't be used at her scheduled trial that week. The Court likely planned to bring Sarah before the Grand Jury and put her on trial as quickly as possible. In many cases, even that of Alice Parker, it was common for people to go to their Grand Jury and Trial on the same day. Mary was likely tried towards the end of the week, as on September 9th, Sarah and Mary wrote a petition to the Court. In this petition, the two sisters asked that the Court allow the counsel to advise them on speaking in their favor. They also asked for several people to be allowed to speak in their defense and not let the testimony of confessed witches be used against them.

~~~

The humble Request of Mary Esty and Sarah Cloyse to the Honoured Court.

Humbly sheweth, that whereas we two Sisters Mary Esty & Sarah Cloyse stand now before the Honoured Court charged with the suspicion of Witchcraft, our humble request is first that seeing we are neither able to plead our own cause, nor is council alowed to those in our condition; that you who are our Judges, would please to be of counsel to us, to direct us where in we may stand in need. Secondly, whereas we are not conscious to ourselves of any guilt in the least degree of that crime, whereof we are now accused (in the presence of the living God we speak it, before whose awful Tribunal we know we shall ere Long appeared) nor of any other scandalous evil, or miscarriage inconsistent with Christianity, Those who have had the Longest and best knowledge of us, being persons of good report, may be suffered to Testify upon oath what they know concerning each of us, viz Mr. Capen the pastor and those of the Town & Church of

Topsfield, who are ready to say something which we hope may be looked upon, as very considerable in this matter; with the seven children of one of us, viz Mary Esty, and it may be produced of Like nature in reference to the wife of Peter Cloyse, her sister. Thirdly, that the testimony of witches, or such as are afflicted, as is supposed, by witches may not be improved to condemn us, without other Legal evidence concurring, we hope the Honoured Court & Jury will be so tender of the lives of such, as we are who have for many years lived under the unblemished reputation of Christianity, as not to condemn them without a fayre and equal hearing of what may be said for us, as well as against us. And your poor suppliants shall be bound always to pray.

~~~

The petition was ignored, although no testimony survives from any confessed witches (unless you count Mary Warren) against Mary Esty. Her Trial is not as well documented as Rebecca's, it was cut and dry, the first of two sittings in September.

Much of the testimony itself related to the dramatics of May 20th and her re-arrest, but much like Rebecca, she received support. Two surviving statements from the Boston Jail Keeper, John Arnold, stated that Mary and Sarah Cloyse were "model prisoners." The Ipswich Jail Keeper Thomas Fosse states that he and his wife Elizabeth saw "no evil carriage." Sarah waited behind as Mary was ferried to and from Salem. During this time, Mary Bradbury and Ann Pudeator were pulled from the Ipswich Jail and tried.

     Mary was found guilty, and Martha Cory, Mary Bradbury, Alice Parker, Ann Pudeator, and Dorcas Hoar were sentenced to hang. Sarah, waiting behind in the Ipswich Jail, anticipated the worst but still prayed to God that a miracle would occur for her sister. Spare her the fate of Rebecca, but when Mary returned to the Ipswich Jail after her trial, she shared the news with Sarah. Thankfully, the Revered Capen did not see the need to embarrass Mary by excommunicating her and damming her soul to all eternity. Having been through this before, Sarah kept Mary close; between family visits and her sister's company, the last few weeks of Mary's life remained peaceful.

~~~

The humble petition of Mary Esty unto His Excellency Sir William Phipps to the honored Judge and Bench now Sitting In Judicature in Salem and the Reverend ministers humbly sheweth

That whereas your poor and humble petitioner being condemned to die do humbly beg of you to take it into your judicious and pious considerations that your poor and humble petitioner knowing my own Innocence Blessed be the Lord for it and seeing plainly the wiles and subtility of my accusers by myself can not but judge charitably of others that are going the same way of my selfe if the Lord stepps not mightily in I was confined a my selfe if the Lord whole month upon the same account that I am condemed now for and then cleared by the same afflicted persons as some of your honours know and in cleared of two days time I was cryed out upon by them and have been confined and now am condemned to die the Lord above knows my Innocencye then and Likewise does now as att the great day will be known to men and Angells -- I Petition to your honours not for my own life for I know I must die and my appointed time is sett but the Lord he knowes it is that if it be possible no more Innocentt blood may be shed which undoubtidly cannot be Avoydd In the way and course you goe in I question not but your honours does to the uttmost of your Powers in the discovery and detecting of witchcraft and witches and would not be gulty of Innocent blood for the world but by my own Innocencye I know you are in the wrong way the Lord in his infinite mercy no more direct you in this great work if it be his blessed will that no more Innocent blood be shed I would humbly begg of you that your honors would be plesed to examine theis Aflicted Persons strictly and keepe them apart some time and Likewise to try some of these confesing wichis I being confident there is severall of them has belyed themselves and others as will appeare if not in this world I am sure in the world to come

whither I am now agoing and I Question not but youle see an alteration of thes things they say my selfe and others having made a League with the Divel will we cannot confesse I know and the Lord knowes as will shortly appeare they belye me and so I Question not but they doe others the Lord above who is the Searcher of all hearts knowes that as I shall answer it att the Tribunal seat that I know not the least thing of Witchcraft, therefore, I cannot I dare not belie my own soul I beg your honers not to deny this my humble petition from a poor dying Innocent person and I Question not but the Lord will give a blessing to your endeavors
To His Excellency Sir William Phipps: Governor and to the honored Judge and Magistrates now setting in Judicature in Salem.

~~~

The petition written on September 15th was not in an effort to save her life but rather to bring to light the proceedings' injustices. She was not the only one of those condemned who submitted a petition to the Court; Ann Pudeator submitted one that stated,

~~~

The humble Petition of Ann Pudeator unto the honored Judge and Bench now Setting in Judicature in Salem humbly sheweth:

That Whereas your Poor and humble Petitioner being condemned to die and knowing in my own conscience as I shall shortly answer it before the great God of heaven who is the searcher & knower of all hearts: That the Evidence of John Best Sen'r and John Best Jun'r and Samuel Pickworth which was given in against me in Court were all of them altogether false & untrue and besides the abovesaid John Best hath been formerly whipped and likewise is recorded for a liar. I would humbly beg of your honors to take it into your Judicious and Pious consideration. That my life may not be taken away by such false evidence and witnesses as these be likewise the evidence given in against me by Sarah

Churchill and Mary Warren. I am altogether ignorant off and know nothing in the least measure about it nor nothing else concerning the crime of Witchcraft for which I am condemned to die as will be known to men and angels at the great day of Judgment, begging and imploring your prayers at the throne of grace in my behalf and your poor and humble petitioner shall forever pray as she is bound in duty for your honors health and happiness in this life and eternal felicity in the world to come.

~~~

Mary Bradbury wrote hers on September 9th, around her trial.

The Answer of Mary Bradbury in the charge of Witchcraft or familliarity with the Devil I doe plead not guilty.
I am wholly innocent of any such wickedness through the goodness of God that have kept me hitherto) I am the servant of Jesus Christ & Have given myself up to him as my only Lord & savior: and to the diligent attendance upon him in all his holy

ordinances, in utter contempt & defiance of the devil, and all his works as horrid & detestable; and accordingly have endeavored to frame my life; & conversation according to the rules of his holy word, & in that faith & practice resolve by the help and assistance of God to continue to my lives end: for the truth of what I say as to matter of practices I humbly refer my self, to my brethren & neighbors that know me and unto the searcher of all hearts for the truth & uprightness of my heart therein (human frailties, & unavoidable infirmities excepted) of which I bitterly complained every day.
Mary Bradbury

~~~

    Regardless of these pleas and petitions, the warrants were signed, and by the end of the 17th, nine more people were tried and condemned: Ann Foster, Mary Lacy Sr, Wilmot Redd, Samuel Wardwell, Margaret Scott, Rebecca Eames, Mary Parker, Abigail Faulkner, and Abigail Hobbs were of those tried. Martha's husband Giles, who stood silent after pleading not guilty, was condemned to *pien-fort-et-dure* due to his silence. He was pressed to death on September 19th in an attempt to break his silence; he was around the age of eighty. The remaining five condemned had to wait as fifteen people couldn't be hanged at once, so around the 17th, a warrant was signed for the executions of Mary Esty, Martha Cory, Mary Bradbury, Alice Parker, Ann Pudeator, Wilmot Redd, Samuel Wardwell, Margaret Scott, Mary Parker, and Dorcas Hoar.

    The Court recessed and made plans to reconvene on November 1st; Sarah likely expected this to be her time to appear before the Court. Sometime between the 10th and 21st of September, Dorcas Hoar tearfully confessed, and the night before her execution, she was granted a one-month temporary reprieve to settle her soul. Mary Bradbury herself would not be present for the hanging as somehow, rather impressively, she successfully escaped from the Ipswich Jail. Albeit likely with financial bribery from the Bradbury family, it's said that Mary hid in Maine until mid-1693 when she returned home to Salisbury.

    In the early morning of September 22nd, the wagon arrived at the Ipswich Jail to take Mary to her execution. Sarah embraced her sister for the final time, walking away from the Jail, and the door closed behind her. Soon, she listened to the rain tapping on the jail roof, likely tucking her legs closer to avoid any leaks from the ceiling. She huddled in the corner, her hands bound by the heavy shackles, waiting for her inevitable fate. Not realizing that the scheduled Court of November 1st would come and go; at the time, no one knew when the Court would sit again; of course, Sarah knew it would be only a matter of time.

Mary's execution was described by Robert Calef in his book More Wonders of the Invisible World written in 1700.

Calef wrote, "*Mary Esty sister also to Rebecca Nurse when she took her last farewell of her husband, children, and friends. Was reported by them present as serious, religious, distinct, and affectionate as could well be expressed. Drawing tears from the eyes of all those present.*"

Chapter 11
Ignoramus

October 1692

There were only a few arrests post-September 22nd, 1692; arrests occurred on September 23rd, October 1st, and November 5th. Not long after the executions, the Quarterly Court reconvened in Ipswich, where in the nearby Sparks Tavern, John Shepard was brought before the Magistrates for his role in helping Mary Green escape. He was fined 5 pounds plus court fees for his role in the breakout. Sarah languished in Ipswich as the Fall grew cold, bundling tight as the night began to frost over on October 9th and light snow on the 10th. The small hearth warmed the prisoners; of course, they were charged for any firewood they would request to be placed there.

The Court of Oyer and Terminer fell on October 29th, with Phips stating it must fall; luckily for them, Lieutenant Governor and Chief Justice of the Court of Oyer and Terminer, William Stoughton, was absent. They had a much more uniform vote with the dispelling of the Court. This led to the November 1st sitting of the Court never happening, giving those in jail hope for release. Three more arrests happened on November 5th. The Governor had banned any arrests for the time being unless in an "unavoidable case," but the Ipswich justice of the peace still issued the warrants to the Gloucester constable.

    Sarah watched as these three women were brought into the Ipswich Jail, showing that nothing had changed as the proceedings had slowed. A new petition was brought forward to the Court, this time from ten people at the Ipswich Jail, asking for a temporary bail to avoid the harsh winter, promising they'd in the Spring to face the courts. The courts ignored this petition, but in the case of Mary Green, who was released on bond in December, things began to look up for some of the accused.

~~~

To the Honourable Governor and Council and General Assembly now sitting at Boston The humble petition of us whose names are subscribed hereunto now prisoners at

Ipswich humbly sheweth that some of us have Lyen in prison many months, and some of us many weeks, who are charged with Witchcraft, and not being conscious to our selves of any guilt of that nature lying upon our consciences; our earnest request is that seeing the winter is so far come on that it can not be expected that we should be tried during this winter season, that we may be released out of prison for the present upon bail to answer what we are charged within the Spring. For we are not in this unwilling nor afraid to abide the tryall before any Judicature appointed in the convenient season of any crime of that nature; we hope you will put on the bowels of compassion so far as to consider of our suffering condition in the present state we are in, being like to perish with cold in lying longer in prison in this cold season of the year, some of us being aged either about or nere four scores some though younger yet being with Child, and one giving suck to a child, not ten weeks old yet, and all of us weak and infirm at best, and one fettered with irons this half year and all most destroyed with soe long an

Imprisonment: Thus hoping you will grant us a release at the present that we are not left to perish in this miserable condition we shall always pray &c.
Widow Penny, Widow Vincent, Widow Prince, Goodwife Green of Haverhill, the wife of Hugh Roe of Cape Anne, Mehitabel Dowing. The wife of Timothy Day, Goodwife Dicer of Piscataqua, Hannah Bromage of Haverhill, Rachel(Clinton) Hafield besides three or four men

~~~

     Sarah, however, was made to wait in the Ipswich Jail, the winter growing colder; having worn the same clothes by this point for around two hundred forty-five days ruined her clothing. Peter brought fresh smocks and perhaps new petticoats or bodices and jackets, but they quickly became soiled, tattered, and insufficient. During the winter, Peter and her children have to surmise that they have supplied more blankets and new stockings for Sarah to combat the cold. Her grip worsened as the cold made her joints ache, with a worry of "*chilblains*" affecting her fingers and toes exposed to the cold.

Finally, in early January 1693, things began to proceed once more to empty the jails of the remaining incarcerated people. The convicted Ann Foster had passed in December of 1692; she was tried in mid-September and sentenced to hang. On January 3rd, 1693, the new Superior Court of Judicature sat in Salem Town at nine o'clock am. The previous Court of Oyer and Terminer was disbanded in October, so the November session did not proceed as planned. The Court would face almost fifty cases of suspected witches in the next fourteen days. Towns all over Essex County provided jurors who would sit and decide the fate of the accused while standing before the Court.

Sarah's former sister-in-law and nieces would stand Trial, with all but one being found not guilty. Many people brought before the Court for their Grand Jury did not make it far; many indicted were returned Ignoramus. Meaning there was insufficient evidence to proceed to trial and all charges were dropped. Rebecca Jacobs, a neighbor of Sarah Cloyse, was one of these people, but she could not be released due to her jail fees. It wouldn't be another month until her release when she borrowed money from a Beverly fisherman to pay her expenses. Many of those who the Court indicted had their cases dismissed, allowing them to be released pending their Jail fees.

    Finally, on January 13th, Sarah was escorted from the Ipswich Jail, traveling through the cold countryside. When arriving in Salem, she climbed the stairs of the Salem Townhouse, the same stairs that led her sisters to their fate. Sarah likely expected her Grand Jury to end in a trial with the same fate as her sisters'. She stood before the Court, recognizing many of the same magistrates from her examination almost a year prior. She stood at the bar while the Magistrates read out the indictments against her, two from her examination on April 11th and the one she received for supposedly afflicting her niece.

    They brought in the afflicted; she was being indicted for tormenting, but as with the twenty-nine others brought before the Grand Jury of the Court of Judicature. The Court returned the three indictments as *ignoramus*, deeming insufficient evidence to hold Sarah for trial. Finally, for once, justice was served in Sarah's eyes; it's unknown when she was released, but likely, her family jumped at the opportunity to save her from the jail. Returning home to her farm in Salem Village likely brought solace to Sarah, who was home with her family, a time for rest and healing. But the scars of her ordeal would last for the remainder of her life.

~~~

  As January turned to February, staying in Salem Village no longer appealed to Sarah and her family. Leaving the Village, the Cloyse family had the opportunity to start a new life far away from the community. The Cloyse family was living in Boston temporarily, likely with his elder children, either Sarah or Peter Jr. During this time, Peter joined his nephews, becoming part of the dissenting group in the Village. Peter, Samuel Nurse, John Tarbell, and Thomas Wilkins came to him to discuss his "unsatisfactory" performance as a minister. This was the beginning of the movement to remove Samuel Parris from his position as Minister of Salem Village.

Peter was invited into Parris's study on the second floor of the Parsonage, allowing him to discuss his thoughts. Parris recorded it in the Church Record Book, in which Parris writes,

"I told them I would go up to my study, asking which would go first, so Brother Cloyce came up first, bringing Bro'r: Way & Tho: Wilkins with him, as witness to his demand of satisfaction to what he lately objected. I told him there was but one Brother, there should be two, Tho: Wilkins was in this case Peter Cloyce, & Peter Cloyce Tho: Wilkins: & so I told the rest, when one saw what they aimed at, & advised them to take according to rule some other Brother, or Brethren, besides Brother Way, or else I could not hear them, in the way they aimed at. But they would urge that this was enough, & one was sufficient; I answered that Christ's rule was for two or three: so they departed."

On February 16th, Thomas Wilkins, John Tarbell, and Samuel Nurse wrote a letter expressing their dissatisfaction, writing,

> "Whereas we, Tho. Wilkins, & John Tarbell, & Samuel Nurse, having a long time gone under the Burden of great grievances by reason of some unwarrantable actings of Mr. Parris, as we esteem them, & were proceeding in an orderly way to obtain satisfaction from him, & had taken some steps thereunto, according to the advice of some neighboring Elders. But obstructive to our proceeding rein, Mr. Parris and some brethren of the Church are appointed by the Church to demand a reason for us withdrawing from communion. The regularity which, the proceeding, we do not understand because, in this case, we esteem selves to be the plaintiffs, and parties offended, & in an orderly way king satisfaction, tho' hitherto denied. Our answer to the Church is that we esteem ourselves hereby prevented in our duty, which [we] account."

Peter would remain involved with the dissenters until around early May of 1693. Throughout the spring and summer, other local ministers became involved in the mediation between the two groups. Parris recorded these interactions in the Church Record Book, writing,

"27. March 1693
At night Bro: Cloyce, Brother Wilkins, & Brother Tarbell abovesaid came to my house at night together with Mr. Joseph Hutchinson, Sen., & Mr. Joseph Putman and a little after William Osburne of Salem (which these last, it seems, came for witnesses, as Bro'r. Cloyce owned the April 20th following) & they gave me a paper not subscribed by any person, but a cut in the place of subscription, where two or three names might be written. The contents of the Paper were as follows: viz. The Paper had no date either.
To our Pastor and Minister, Mr. Sam Parris of Salem Village, & to some others of the plantation.
Wee whose names are underwritten, being deeply sensible that those uncomfortable differences that are amongst us are very dishonorable to God, & a scandal to Religion, & very uncomfortable to ourselves, & of an ill example to those that

may come after us. And by our maintaining & upholding differences amongst us, we do but gratify the Devil, that grand adversary of our Souls. For the Removal of which we have thought to meet to proffer our present thoughts for your serious consideration, hoping that there may be such methods propounded as may be for the settling & confirming peace & unity amongst us both at present & for the future. And our desires are that such a foundation may be laid for peace and truth that the gates of Hell may not prevail against it. And in order thereunto Solomon adviseth to Counsell. And we desire that a council of Elders may be mutually chosen to hear all our grievances between Mr. Parris and us and determine the blamable cause. And we hope that their wisdom & prudence may direct us to such a method, as may be for our comfort, for both present and future.

When I had read it, I asked them where this Paper came from. They answered all the Plantations or at least many of them. One demanded why none subscribed to it. They said, all in good time. So I put it in my pocket. They demanded an answer. I told them one would consider it.

"28. March. 1693
The abovesaid Brethren, together with said Hutchinson, came again at night for an answer to the abovesaid Paper: I told them one had not considered of it yet."

"14. April. 1693
Our displeased Brethren, Jno: Tarbell, Sam: Nurse, and Tho: Wilkins came in, bringing with them, said Hutchinson and Francis Nurse. After a little while, I went down from my study to them, asking them if they would speak with me. Icy said yes, and they came to discourse about the Paper (abovesaid) they had ought to me. I told them I had no time to talk. I was there that day to preach at a private meeting. Nor was one willing to discourse with them alone, but I would appoint me a place to meet with them. So we agreed after our next Lecture to meet at Bro. Nathaniel Putman's."

"20. April. 1693
After the Lecture, Capt. Putnam, Ensign Flint, & the two Deacons met the four displeased Brethren abovesaid at Lt. Nath. Putnams abovesaid, where we found

together with them, & for them said Mr. Hutchinson & Mr. Israel Porter. After a little while, I told them to gratify them, and I was able to hear what they had to offer. They demanded an answer to the Paper above. Whereupon I plucked it out of my pocket, & read it openly. They owned that it be the Paper. I asked them what they called it. They begin to seek a name for it. I told them I looked upon it as a Libel. Then they produced a like paper subscribed by said Brethren and divers more to the number of forty and two names, but all seemed to be one & the same hand. I desired the original Paper; they said they did not know where it was. Then, it was asked whether those men used their own names. It was answered yes, or they were written by their order. Then I desired them to subscribe to this Paper with their hands, testifying that no name was there, but such as had consulted thereto. But none would yield to this. Then I told them we must know, what we do. Had I to deal with displeased People, or displeased Brethren? They answered, they came as Brethren. Then I told them none but Brethren should have been present. They said they had been with me already, & I refused to give them satisfaction. I answered that I did not understand their drift and, & therefore, did not discourse them, as I would have done had I apprehended they came to reason as such as had taken offense. And when they came the second time they brought but one Brother viz: William Way, & took others of themselves.

Lt. Putman told them it was not too late yet, now there were several of the Brethren [present], & they might take any two of them, & discourse with the Pastor. No, they said they had done it already. Thus much time was spent till just night; & myself and other Brethren upon going home: the 4. displeased Brethren agreed to meet me tomorrow morning about an hour after sunrise, with the two Deacons and Bro'r. William Way & Brother Aaron Way, to discourse the matter to which I readily assented."

"21. April. 1693
This morning, we met as said at Deacon Ingersolls. After a little while, I began praying. Then, Brother Nurse read a large scroll of about fifteen articles as reasons why they withdrew communion from us. 7. of

them, I think, were reasons for absenting from public worship with us, & the other eight, I think, were causes of separation from my Ministry. I desired to see them, but was denied for a great while. At length, I had the liberty to read them myself upon the promise of returning them to them. After all, I demanded them or a copy of them. But they would not consent thereto: nor to the desire of the other four indifferent Brethren: tho' we urged it by argument. But the Dissenters said no: They had told me, & that was enough, and they desired me to call the Church, & then I should have it."

*"Sab: 30. Apr. 1693
After public worship ended, the Church stayed, to whom the Pastor spoke. To this effect, Brethren, you know some of our Brethren have withdrawn from us for a time. One do not understand their Methods. They desire to speak with the Church; if you gratify them herein, I recommend their motion to you. After a bit of discourse, it was voted that the Church meet on May 18th next, after the Lecture, at the Pastor's house, and in the meantime, Brother Benj. Putman and Bro. Sam Sibly to acquaint Bro: Nurse*

and Bro. Tarbell tomorrow (Bro. Cloyes being at Boston, where he has lived these many months; so that we sent not to him, supposing the abovesaid his kinsmen would); and Bro. Benj. Wilkins and Bro. Aaron Wey will also acquaint their neighbor Tho: Wilkins tomorrow so that they all have timely notice."

While the group was meeting and debating with Parris, the Cloyses remained in Boston. Sarah likely spent many months recuperating in the home she stayed in, although many of the hearings for the remaining accused in a *Not Guilty* verdict or the cases were dismissed. The unease of being accused remained, and Sarah nearly fell victim to the Court of Oyer, and Terminer remained on high alert. Three people were convicted and sentenced to hang outside, remaining convicted from the September Trials in 1692. But Phips reprieved them at the last minute, and as a result, no more people were hanged in the Massachusetts Bay Colony for the crime of Witchcraft. Unfortunately, Sarah would never know in her lifetime; as quickly as they came, the trials would end. But, as no more accusations sprung up, Sarah likely felt more at peace slowly as time passed.

~~~

An opportunity came from an unknown source for Sarah and her family to settle in a new community they could help build. Making the journey west into more frontier land was unnerving for anyone, reminding the Cloyse family of the rural Salem Village. They arrived in Sudbury, a small community West of Boston, founded in 1639. It was large and not densely populated. Somehow, Peter had purchased a plot of land in the community; the transaction was lost to history. The new property was only a few thousand feet west of Cowassock Brook in the area known as "*Danforth Farms*," land owned by Thomas Danforth, the same man who had witnessed Sarah's examination in mid-April of the previous year.

Whether Thomas gave the land to them is unknown, but it was here Peter and Sarah essentially rebuilt their lives after the 1692 Witch Trials. Joining them were Sarah's children Benjamin, Hannah, Caleb,

Alice, and John, Peter's children Peter Jr and John, and their daughter Hepzibah. Further extended family included her nephew Benjamin Nurse, and more members of Sarah and Peter's extended families joined them as they began to rebuild their lives. The home built in the area now known as "*Salem End Road*" has since been lost to history; however, the house located on the spot likely shares the original's foundation. The original 1693 home was likely a two-room house with a lean-to in the back and Garrett space in the lean-to attic. The home would've been simple, as would've been many of the early homes in the area, such as those of her nephew Benjamin and son Caleb.

    The trauma Sarah faced in jail is something no one should ever have to go through; hearing the wails and moans of those people who surrounded her would fill her ears for the rest of her life. The thought of her sisters, watching both of them being taken from her to their deaths, each time knowing that she was closer and closer to the hangman's noose, terrified her. Time heals all wounds, but the memory remains of what Sarah went through; she watched as twenty-five people left the Jail and lost their lives from hanging, pressing, or simply the terrible conditions. However, as shown in the surviving records, Sarah had the support of her husband and family to carry her through those dark days as they did during 1692.

In December of that first year in "*Danforth Farms*," Sarah's stepson, Peter, married her grandniece, Mary Preston. As the family grew, the ties to Salem Village waned; in 1695, Peter and Sarah's church membership was transferred to the Marlborough Church nearby. That same year, Rebecca's widower, Francis Nurse, passed away around the age of seventy-eight, and his farm was passed onto his son Samuel. Life moved forward, her children grew, and soon, grandchildren filled Sarah's heart as her children and stepchildren grew. News spread to the Cloyse family in 1696 that Parris had finally left Salem Village and was replaced by John Green. The actions of Peter's early role and the ongoing effort of nephews and friends in the Village had worked. Finally, Parris was gone. In 1698, Peter joined a group in Sudbury that wished for the "*Danforth Farms*" area to separate into its community.

    His efforts were successful, and by August 5th of 1700, Peter *Clayes* became one of the founding selectmen of Framingham. His role was not forgotten, and within the next few years, his rank in the Town increased, allowing Sarah to enjoy some comfort with his new role. In March 1701, Peter was elected Town Treasurer and Grand juryman. His newfound wealth allowed the family to expand the smaller two-room house and lean-to into a four-room house, a much larger and more spacious option for the large family full of children and grandchildren. As Sarah aged, her daughters Alice and Hepzibah would've picked up the more matronly roles of cooking, gardening, and any chores Sarah could no longer do.

    With Peter's help, a new Meeting House was built in Framingham, allowing those who lived nearby to attend Meetings here rather than in Marlborough. Thirty feet by forty feet, two stories high with large double doors facing south, each side having men's and women's pews and galleys accessed by stairs in the southwest and southeast corners. Pews were located against the walls on the first floor, and benches filled the middle aisle of the Meeting House, all facing the pulpit, which stood facing North. Soon, Sarah and Peter's church membership was transferred from Marlborough to Framingham in October of 1701. The memberships of her sons Benjamin and Caleb, as well as her nephew Benjamin, also followed at the same time.

  Sarah enjoyed relative comfort in her final years, surrounded by her family and her husband, who had supported her through the past ten years of pain and healing. Around sixty-two, Sarah took her last breath, passing away at some point in 1703, leaving behind her husband, children, and grandchildren. The horrors Sarah faced likely had never fully healed, her pain and suffering only being healed in death and resting with the comfort of her soul making its way into Heaven to be with her family and her sisters that were taken from her. One of God's chosen to spend eternity in Heaven, much like Sarai, who was renamed "*Sarah*" when she was to fulfill her destiny to give Abraham a son.

Sarah, fulfilled her destiny, becoming a strong woman, mother, and grandmother. She was blessed to become the *Mother of Nations* by helping her husband settle and incorporate Framingham. Her line continued on to found the American Red Cross through her third great-granddaughter, Clara Barton. Sarah was laid to rest in a now-lost grave, but perhaps one has to wonder if that is how Sarah wants it to be—allowing her peace in the afterlife, which she had waited so long for.

~~~

Peter remarried in 1704 to the widow Susannah (Harrington) Beers, not to discredit his marriage to Sarah but rather as a necessity. He lived only a few more years, passing away on July 18th, 1708; his will was signed only a few days earlier. He left behind many items to his surviving wife and his children and stepchildren;

To his widow, he left "*her movable estate, one cow and the best and largest swine, all provision in the house, 20 bushels of Indian Corn, ⅓ improvement of my lands and* continual income and profit and a suitable and convenient room in the dwelling house as long as she remains my widow."

To his daughter Mary, "*Well-beloved daughter Mary Trumball, four pounds and a feather bed with all the furniture thereunto belonging, which said the bed was my daughter's Mother's bed, to wit. Hannah Clayes.*"

To his daughter Hannah Eliot, he left five pounds.

To his daughter Hepzibah Harrington, "*Standing cupboard which was her Mother, Sarah Clayes.*"

To his granddaughter Abigail Waters, "*Forty shillings in money or goods when she comes of age.*"

To his grandchildren, "*To my well beloved grand child[ren] six pounds in money or goods at money price, to be equally divided betwixt them and to be paid unto them as they shall come of age.*"

To his stepdaughter Alice Bridges: "*A flock bed and a large pewter platter which was her Mothers, to wit, Sarah Clayes.*"

He left instructions to his executors: "*During the present circumstances of my said daughter's* [Mary Trumball's likely] *single life, find her a convenient shop-room for the occupation or trade of a weaver in my old house and also a convenient house room to dwell and lodge in, plus a cow.*" His estate was divided between his sons Peter and James, and the inventory was taken on July 23rd and exhibited on August 17th, 1708.

~~~

    Around the time of Sarah's death in 1703, the first exonerations would take place for Elizabeth Proctor, Sarah Wardwell, and Abigail Faulkner, with efforts moving forward to exonerate Rebecca, Mary, Mary Parker, John Procter, Elizabeth How, and Samuel Wardwell as well. A 1703 petition was signed by Peter, Isaac Esty Sr, Isaac Esty Jr, Samuel Nurse, John Tarbell, John Nurse, and Rebecca Preston in support of the family of the others mentioned in it. It wasn't until 1711 when the Court cleared Mary and Rebecca of all charges alongside George Burroughs, John Proctor, George Jacobs, John Willard, Giles and Martha Cory, Sarah Wildes, Abigail Hobbs, Samuel Wardwell, Mary Parker, Martha Carrier, Ann Foster, Rebecca Eames, Mary Post, Mary Lacy Sr, Mary Bradury, and Dorcas Hoar were cleared. Further restitution was provided to the families as compensation for visiting their family members in jail. Had Peter lived until 1712 or later, he would likely have sought financial compensation for Sarah's incarceration, but as we cannot answer for the dead, it's unknown.

~~~

In short, Sarah Cloyse fought for her life, working with her family to find a way out, and she succeeded. Her story is one of ups and downs, but she made it through it all. She is truly a woman of great strength and means. For years, she was relegated to the third sister or the subject of misconceptions and forgotten stories, but through it all, one thing is sure, she was "Super Sarah"

Authors Note and Acknowledgments

I first decided to research for a book regarding the Witch Trials several years ago. When I learned of my own connection to the events through my ancestor Susannah Roots of Beverly. It bounced around several people before I had settled on Sarah. I knew I didn't have the skill set to write both a narrative and scholarly text. So, I decided to simply tell Sarah's story through a semi narrative biography. I started writing the book on January 13th, 2024 the 331st anniversary of Sarah's freedom and finished on May 27th, 2024 on the 39th anniversary of *Three Sovereigns for Sarah*.

Two years of research culminated in five months of writing. Learning about the trials it self and then only focusing on Sarah's story was the only way to do it. I learned things that most people had never known, how connected Sarah is to so many people from all aspects of the Trials. While *Three Sovereigns* is not 100% accurate, it allowed for her story to be told. It's what inspired me to write a book in the first place, to tell a story using primary source documents. The only assumptions made are those made logically based on human emotion and reason.

 My amazing Mother listened to me drone on about the Trials and still willingly read the chapters as I finished them. My Nana who listed to my phone calls as I ranted about the Trials and it's history. My best friends Adriana and Indie who just simply listened to me, and to Adriana for designing the cover of this book and future books. I also have the privilege to be a volunteer at the Rebecca Nurse Homestead to tell Rebecca's true story alongside Sarah and Mary's. I do wish I told Mary's story more in depth here, perhaps for a future book I'll tackle hers and take a more in depth look to the September Trials.

 I want to thank Candice and Kathryn for theorizing with me about different aspects of the Towne sisters life. Thank you to Lisa Trask and Krystina Yeager for edits and a big thank you to the Rebecca Nurse Homestead crew and the Danvers Alarm List Company for taking me in and allowing me to yap on and on. To Mary, Josh, and Sarah and the Massachusetts Witch Hunt Exoneration Project crew, to giving me the motivation and inspiration to keep writing. The Topsfield Library and Framingham Historical Society for providing me with the needed research to tell Sarah's story. To Richard Trask and Julie Silk you helped provide a much needed background and gave an idea on what happened in Sarah's life before and during 1692. To Marilynne Roach, your work helped me streamline and polish the daily nature of the Trials, breaking any preconceived notions I may have had. To my friend Tasha for even inspiring me to write in general thank you dearly. I cannot thank everyone because then this book will be 10,000 pages long.

I appreciate all of you more than you'll ever know <3

Endnotes

I decided to break down the notes into each topic I discussed in each chapter. The following below are some of the abbreviations used for the Endnotes.

- EQC: Essex County Quarterly Court Records
- SV-CR: Salem Village Church Records
- ST-CR: Salem Town Church Records
- Salem VR: Salem Vital Records

Chapter 1
- The Marriage of William and Joanna Towne: St. Nicholas Parish Register [note 1]; William Towne and Joanna Blessing married April 25, 1620, Hoover, Towne Family, 2
- The Towne's leaving Yarmouth: Hoover, Towne Family, 2, *Norwich Consistory & Archdeaconry Visitation Records*
- Early Salem:
  - The Area: Massachusetts Historical Commission. "MHC Reconnaissance Survey Town

Report: Salem" (PDF). *Mass Historical Commission,* Phippen, George D. "Old Planters of Salem" *Hist. Coll. of the Essex Institute* Vol. 1, 97 et seq, Perley, *The History of Salem Massachusetts,* 316, George Francis Dow, *Every Day Life in the Massachusetts Bay Colony,* 16-17, 20-21

- Meeting House and Puritan Beliefs: Perley, *History of Salem,* 1:257, Perley, *History of Salem,* 2:82, Perley, *History of Salem,* 2:83, George Francis Dow, *Every Day Life in the Massachusetts Bay Colony,* 102
- Clothing: George Francis Dow, *Every Day Life in the Massachusetts Bay Colony,* 94
- Sumptuary Laws: Massachusetts; Shurtleff, Nathaniel B. (Nathaniel Bradstreet); Court, Massachusetts General (1854). *Records of the governor and company of the Massachusetts Bay in New England.* William

White, Printer to the Commonwealth, EQC 1:303
- The Towne Family
  - Sarah's Birth: EQC VII pg 249-250, Salem Village Church Records, p. 3
  - Bible Verse of the name Rebecca: Genesis 24:60 KJV
  - Rebecca's Marriage: Clarance Almon Torrey, New England Marriages Prior to 1700 (Baltimore Genealogical Publishing Co., 1985), 541
  - First Record of Francis Nurse: EQC, 1:16
  - Rebecca's Children: Hoover, *Towne Family,* 9-10
  - Joanna Church Membership and Sarah and Joseph Baptism: Pierce, *The Records of the First Church of Salem,* 22
  - Rebecca Church Membership: Peirce, *The Records of the First Church of Salem,* 127
  - Sarah Church Membership: Salem Village Church Record page 3

- Towne Farm in Topsfield: Hoover, *Towne Family,* 2
- Edmund Marriage and Children: Hoover, *Towne Family,* 103-105
- Mary (Towne) Esty Marriage and Children: Hoover, *Towne Family,* 263
- Jacob Towne Marriage: Hoover, *Towne Family,* 183-184, *Topsfield VRs [note 2],* 1:193; Towne, Jacob to Katheren Symons, June 26, 1657. [ECQR]
- The Bridges Family
  - Edmund Bridges Sr: *Great Migration 1634-1635, A-B.* Pages 389-392
  - Sarah and Edmund Bridges Marriage: Hoover, *Towne Family,* 398
  - Bridges Topsfield Farm: Dow, *History of Topsfield Massachusetts,* 34
  - Common Land Portions: Dow, *History of Topsfield Massachusetts,* 54

Chapter 2
- Daily life of the typical Puritan Family

- Dow, *Every Day Life in the Massachusetts Bay Colony*, 20-21
- Unknown "Sister" Case, 1664:
  - EQC 3:138
  - McMillen, *Currents of Malice*, 72
- Gould Family of Topsfield
  - Gould, *Zaccheus Gould of Topsfield*, 9
  - Dow, *History of Topsfield Massachusetts*, 54
- Blacksmithing in Colonial New England
  - Bernard Bailyn, *The New England Merchants in the Seventeenth Century*, 61
- Edmund v. John Gould
  - EQC 4:293
  - EQC 4:170- This refers to a case on April 23rd, 1669 but nothing is further recorded, there is also a case between Edmund and William Averill for not paying William Browne in "malt, wheat, and Indian corn"
  - Ibid 4:293
  - Ibid 4:294

- Ibid 4: 295
* Bridges Family in Salem Town
  - Perley, History of Salem, 2:355
* Passing of William Towne
  - Hoover, *Towne Family,* 3-4
* Site of Bridges Family Home
  - Essex Antiquarian (1906, p.30-31), Sydney Perley, Salem in 1700 Map.
* 17th Century Taverns Useage and Laws
  - Russell Hawes Kettell, Editor, Early American Rooms The Southworth-Anthoensen Press, Portland, Maine, 1936, p. 85.
  - Faveretti and DeWolf, p. 11-12
  - Field, p. 12-13
  - Anna Fox Toogood, A Comparative Study: Ephraim Hartwell Tavern, Minute Man National Historical Park, Massachusetts, p. 28-29
* Edward and Sarah Bishop Tavern
  - EQC 9:517
* Merchant's in Salem
  - Sydney Perley, Salem in 1700 Map, Charles F. Caroll, *The Timber Economy of Puritan New*

England, Providence, Rhode Island, 1973
- New Salem Town Meeting House
  - Perley, History of Salem, 2:430-431
- Edmund Bridges v. Edmund Batter
  - EQC 7:32
  - Ibid 7:32-33
  - Ibid 7:33

Chapter 3
- Higginson's Petition against Illegal Taverns
  - EQC 7:71
- Higginson against Edmund Bridges
  - Ibid 7:72
- Edmund and Sarah are fined for breaking Tavern operation laws
  - Ibid 7:72
  - Ibid 7:80
  - Ibid 7:81
- John Proctor v. Giles Cory
  - EQC 7:89-91
  - Ibid 7:90
- Edmund Attorney Cases
  - EQC 7:93, 100
- Quaker Patron
  - Ibid 7:110
- Edmund being brought to court

- Ibid 7:111-114
- Ibid 7:141
- Ibid 7:146
- Ibid 7:315
- Bridget and Thomas Oliver
  - EQC 6:386-387
- Thomas Maul v. James Brown
  - EQC 7:249-250
- Edmund and Sarah's new seats in the Meeting House
  - Perley, *History of Salem*, 2:33

Chapter 4
- Will of Edmund Bridges Jr
  - *Essex Co. Probate, Old Series*, vol 2:23
- Edmund Bridges Jr Marriage to Elizabeth Croade
  - *Essex Co. Probate, Old Series*, vol 2:23
- Death of Edmund Bridges Sr
  - *Essex Co. Probate, Old Series*, vol. 2:32
  - Hoover, 398
- Death of Edmund Towne
  - Hoover, *Towne Family*, 103
- Sarah's removal from Topsfield
  - Dow, *History of Topsfield*, pg. 344

- Joanna Towne Death
  - Hoover, *Towne Family,* 3-4
- Peter Cloyse early life and first Marriage
  - Holman; *Genealogical Dictionary of Maine and New Hampshire-* p.152
  - Hoover, *Towne Family,* 398
  - Peirce, *The Records of the First Church of Salem, 32-33*: Sarah, Hannah, Peter, and Mary were baptized in 1676, listed as "of Peter Clois of York". James is baptized in 1679, listed as "of Peter Cloye" disregarding the lack of standardized spelling these are Peter's first five children.
  - Edmund and Peter: EQC 6:386
- Sarah's Marriage to Peter
  - Hoover, *Towne Family,* 398
- Benoni Cloyse
  - Salem VR, 1:188; Cloys, Benoni, s. P. Bp. Sept, 2, 1683. [CR, First Church of Salem]
- Cloyse property in Salem Village
  - Boyer, Nissenbaum, *Salem Possessed,* 182

- Hepzibah Cloyse
  - Hoover, *Towne Family,* 400
- Death of Mary Jacobs
  - EQC 9:517
- Dominion of New England
  - Barth, Jonathan Edward (2014). "'A Peculiar Stampe of Our Owne': The Massachusetts Mint and the Battle over Sovereignty, 1652-1691". *The New England Quarterly.*
- Goody Glover Case
  - Cotton Mather, *Memorable Provinces,* 1689
- Samuel Parris arrival
  - Gragg, Larry (1990). *A Quest for Security: The Life of Samuel Parris, pp. 45-46*
- Sarah's Church Membership
  - SV-CR p. 3

Chapter 5
- Misinformation of Voodoo and other causes of the Trials
  - Upham, Salem, 2:2-6
- Phips Appointed Governor and new Charter
  - C. Mather, Magnalia (1977), 322
- Tituba is visited by the Devil

- Rosenthal, Records of the Salem Witch Hunt, Doc 3
  - Doc. 6
  - Doc. 3
- Sarah Good visits the Parsonage
  - Doc. 3
- Charter arrives
  - Sewall, p. 356
- Thomas Putnam Sr. will
  - Suffolk County, MA: Probate File Papers, Will of Thomas Putnam Sr.
- The afflicted diagnosis
  - Hale, 23; Calef Burr, 342; SV Church Records, Mar. 27, C. Mather *Memorable Provinces*; Burr, 104; I. Mather, *Remarkable Provinces*; Burr, 21-23
- Counter magic
  - Hale 23-25; Lawson Brief and True, 162-163
  - K. Thomas 437-438, 543-544
- Goody Glover
  - Hale, 24
  - Ibid, 25
- First Accusations and Arrests
  - Doc. 1
  - Ibid. 2

- Ibid. 7
- Ibid. 9
- Ibid. 10
- Sarah Osbourne's legal Issues
  - Rosenthal, Records of the Salem Witch Hunt, Doc. 5, Doc. 6; Boyer, *Salem Possessed,* 193-194; Essex Probate 308: 228-229
- Weather around Feb. 29 1692
  - Sewall *Diary* Feb 27. 1692
- Sarah Good Examination
  - Doc. 3
- Sarah Osbourne Examination
  - Ibid. 3
- Tituba Examination
  - Ibid. 3, 6

Chapter 6
- Martha Cory suspected, arrested, examined
  - Rosenthal, Records of the Salem Witch Hunt, Docs. 15, 16, 18
- Rebecca Nurse suspected
  - Ibid. 35, 291
- Israel and Elizabeth Porter, Daniel Andrew's, and Peter Cloyse visit
  - Ibid. 31
- Rebecca's arrest and examination

- ○ Ibid. 23, 28
- Dorothy Good arrest, imprisonment, and examination
  - ○ Ibid. 22, 25, 858
- Spectral Evidence usage at the Bury of St. Edmunds Witch Trial
  - ○ Notestein 1911, p. 261-262, 264
  - ○ Clark 1838, p. 11
- Yellow Birds
  - ○ Lawson, A Brief and True Narritive, 154
- Salem Jail
  - ○ Nantucket Historical Association, *"The Old Gaol"* this jail was built in 1805 but was similar in size and style to that of the jail in Salem https://nha.org/wp-content/uploads/History-of-Old-Gaol.pdf
- Sarah storms from the Meeting House
  - ○ Lawson, A Brief and True Narritive, 160, 161, Rosenthal, Records of the Salem Witch Hunt, Doc. 49, Doc. 244

Chapter 7
- Testimony against Elizabeth:
  - ○ Rosenthal, Records of the Salem Witch Hunt Doc. 61

- Complaint and Arrest of Sarah Cloyse and Elizabeth Proctor
    - Rosenthal, Records of the Salem Witch Hunt Doc. 39
    - S. Noyes 429-430
- John Indian's testimony against Sarah Cloyse
    - Rosenthal, Records of the Salem Witch Hunt Doc. 49
- Testimony against Rebecca Nurse, Martha Corey, Sarah Good, and Sarah Cloyse
    - Doc. 48
- Salem Town Meeting House
    - Perley, History of Salem, 2:430-431
- Examination of Sarah Cloyse and Elizabeth Proctor
    - Doc. 39
    - Ibid. 47
    - Ibid. 49
    - Sewall, Diary, April 11, 1692 p. 358
    - Upham, *Salem Witchcraft,* p. 386-388; Upham is an unreliable source, but as he wrote the book in the 1850s he had access to

documents no longer available to us.
- Arrest of John Proctor from the Examination
    - Doc. 49
- Testimony aginst John Proctor
    - Ibid. 69
- Imprisonment of Sarah Cloyse, John Proctor, and Elizabeth Proctor
    - Ibid. 47, 216, 217, 612
- Map of Boston, c. 1676
    - Samuel C. Clough, Map of the Town of Boston, 1676 (Boston, 1920), MHS Collections Online, https://www.masshist.org/database/viewer.php?item_id=1737&img_step=1&br=1&mode=zoomify#page1: this map details the passage Sarah and the others took to the Jail from the Ferry site.
- Boston Jail
    - Foote. Annals of King's Chapel from the Puritan age of New England to the present day, Volume 1. Boston: Little, Brown, 1900; p.86

- Death of John and Hannah Putnam's baby
  - Rosenthal, *Records of the Salem Witch Hunt*, Doc. 362

Chapter 8
- Arrest of Mary Esty and others
  - Rosenthal, Records of the Salem Witch Hunt, Doc. 79
- Examination of Mary Esty
  - Doc. 86
- Testimony against Mary Esty from her Examination
  - Doc. 87
  - Ibid. 88
- Prison Transfers of George Jacobs Sr, Giles Cory, William Hobbs, Edward and Sarah Bishop, Bridget Bishop, Sarah Wildes, Mary Black, Mary English, Alice Parker, and Ann Pudeator
  - Ibid. 216
- Other Prisoners in the Salem Jail
  - Ibid. 216
- The retrieval of Ann Putnam Jr and Abigail Williams and Esty's specter following them
  - Ibid. 206
  - Ibid. 204

- Description of Mercy Lewis's condition
  - Ibid. 205
  - Ibid. 204
- More specters attack
  - Ibid. 197
- Second Arrest Warrant of Mary Esty
  - Ibid. 187
- Further testimony against Mary Esty from the event on May 20th, 1692
  - Ibid. 191, 206, 195, 196, 197, 203, 204, 209, 213, 216, 224
- Reincarceration of Mary Esty
  - Ibid. 216

Chapter 9
- Salem Village touch test and arrest of Elizabeth Cary
  - Rosenthal, Records of the Salem Witch Hunt, Doc. 203
- Death of Sarah Osbourne
  - Ibid. 858
- Arrival of the Charter and the establishment of the Court of Oyer and Terminer
  - Sewall Diary, May 14th, 1692, Council, 176; D. C. Brown *Forfeitures,* 88-89; Note: The court name "Oyer and Terminer"

means to "Hear and determine" in Latin
- Rebecca is sent back to the Salem Jail pending her Grand Jury
    - Doc. 253
- Petition of Isreal Porter for Rebecca Nurse
    - Ibid. 254
- Sarah Holten Testimony against Rebecca
    - Ibid. 358
- Summons of witnesses for Rebecca's Grand Jury
    - Ibid. 259
- Depostion of Ann Putnam Sr against Rebecca Nurse, Sarah Cloyse, Sarah Bishop, and Elizabeth Cary
    - Ibid. 267
- Indictments against Rebecca Nurse
    - Ibid. 285, 286, 287, 288
- Physical Examination of Rebecca Nurse and her Daughter's statements
    - Ibid. 271 and 294
- Execution of Bridget Bishop
    - Ibid. 313
- Transfer of Sarah Cloyse, Mary Esty, George Burroughs, George Jacobs Sr, Giles and Martha Cory, Ann Pudeator,

Sarah Wildes, Susannah Roots, and Dorcas Hoar
  - Ibid. 841
  - Mass. Archives 40:622
  - Roach, *Salem Witch Trials,* 173
- Deposition of Sarah Stephens and Margery Pasque against Rebecca Nurse, Sarah Cloyce, & Faith Black
  - Doc. 343
- Depostion of John Putnam Jr and Hannah Putnam against Rebecca Nurse, Mary Esty, and Sarah Cloyse
  - Ibid. 362
- Testimony used at the Trial of Rebecca Nurse
  - Ibid. 343, 357-373, and 382
- Sarah Nurse against Sarah Bibber
  - Ibid. 367
- Statement of Rebecca Nurse on July 3rd, 1692
  - Ibid. 417
- Statement of Thomas Fiske
  - Ibid. 416
- Excommunication of Rebecca Nurse
  - Peirce, *The Records of the First Church of Salem,* 172
- Reprieve of Rebecca Nurse and revoking of reprieve

- ○ Calef, *More Wonders*, p. 103
- Death Warrant for Rebecca Nurse, Sarah Good, Sarah Wildes, Elizabeth Howe, and Susannah Martin
  - ○ Doc. 418

Chapter 10
- Accusations spread to Andover, arrests of Mary Lacy Sr and Jr
  - ○ Ibid. 421, 422
- Arrest of Sarah's sister-in-law Mary (Tyler) Bridges Sr
  - ○ Ibid. 437
- Marriage of Mary Tyler to John Bridges
  - ○ Anderson, The Great Migration Begins: Immigrants to New England, 1620-1633, Volumes 1-3; p 391
- Arrest of Mary Green and Hannah Bromage and Examination of Hannah Bromage
  - ○ Doc. 438, 440
- Indictment of Hannah Bromage for afflicting Mary Walcott
  - ○ Ibid. 807
- Sarah Cloyse, Mary Esty, Hannah Bromage, and Mary Green are sent to the Ipswich Jail

- ○ Ibid. 552, 870, SV-CR p. 12
- Ipswich Jail and Prisoners Work
  - ○ Waters, Thomas Franklin: Ipswich in the Massachusetts Bay Colony, Vol. 1, p. 427, 428
  - ○ Early incarcerated prisoners when it was originally built in the 1650s. It's possible however they kept this by 1692 to give the accused something to do, the Boston Jail was known to send its prisoners to work houses as well. Or at least provide work inside the prison for inmates to do while incarcerated.
- Absence of Peter Cloyse, Samuel Nurse and many other members of the Nurse Family
  - ○ SV-CR p. 12
- Escape of Mary Green
  - ○ Doc. 678, 855
- Mary Esty Grand Jury Indictments
  - ○ Doc. 459, 460
- Further arrests of Mary Clark, Margaret Scott, Elizabeth Johnson Jr, Sarah and Thomas Carrier, Abigail Faulkner

- Ibid. 450, 451, 505, 503, 504, 506, 507
- Physical Examination of Sarah Cloyse and Mary Esty
  - Ibid. 869
  - Calef, *More Wonders of the Invisible World,* 107
- Summons for Witnesses against Sarah Cloyse, Mary Esty, Giles and Martha Cory
  - Ibid. 549
- Summons for Witnesses against Sarah Cloyse and Mary Esty
  - Ibid. 554
- Excuse of Mary Towne
  - Ibid. 576
- Summons for Mary and Rebecca Towne
  - Ibid. 579
- Indictment for Sarah Cloyse for afflicting Rebecca Towne
  - Ibid. 809
- Petition of Sarah Cloyse and Mary Esty
  - Ibid. 596
- Mary Esty Convicted
  - Calef, Burr, 366

- Support for Sarah Cloyse and Mary Esty
  - Ibid. 552, 602
- Petition of Mary Esty
  - Ibid. 654
- Petition of Ann Pudeator
  - Ibid. 655
- Statement of Mary Bradbury
  - Ibid. 597
- Pressing of Giles Cory
  - Sewall *Diary* Sep. 19 1692, Calef, Burr, 367, Doc. 899
- Reprieve of Dorcas Hoar
  - Doc. 676
- September Executions
  - Calef, *More Wonders of the Invisible World,* 107

Chapter 11
- Gloucester Arrests
  - Rosenthal, Records of the Salem Witch Hunt, Doc. 702, Mehitable Downing was arrested from Gloucester on September 23rd, no record of arrest survives only imprisment. On October 1st: Mary Row, Rachel Vinson, and Phebe Day of Gloucester were

arrested, no warrant surives only imprisonment.
- Rosenthal, Records of the Salem Witch Hunt, Doc. 704: On November 5th: Esther Elwell, Abigail Row, and Rebecca Dike of Gloucester were arrested.
- John Shepard for Assisting in the escape of Mary Green
  - Doc. 678
- Displusion of the Court of Oyer and Terminer
  - Sewall, *Diary,* Oct. 29, 1692
- Release of Mary Green
  - Ibid. 702, 723
- Court of Judicature begins, Superior Court of Judicature Record Book: Court of Assize and General Jail Delivery Held at Salem, Essex County
  - Ibid. 747, Middlesex Court Records, 158
- Trials of Mary Bridges and her daughters
  - Docs. 796, 797, 798, 799, 847, and 849
- Grand Jury of Rebecca Jacobs
  - Doc. 752
- Moving to Boston from Salem Village

- SV-CR p. 15: Referred to Peter as coming from Boston.
- Dissenting Group of Salem Village
  - SV-CR. p 15
  - SV-CR. p. 15-16
  - SV-CR. p. 16
  - SV-CR. p. 16-17
  - SV-CR. p. 17
- Moving to Sudbury and Danforth Farms
  - Howard, *History of Framingham*, 108
- Marriage of Peter Cloyse Jr to Mary Preston
  - Ibid. p. 507
- Sarah and Peter Church Membership transfer
  - SV-CR p. 32
- Death of Francis Nurse
  - The New England Historical and Genealogical Register, Volume 13, New England Historic Genealogical Society Boston, Massachusetts, 1859, p. 56
- Peter Cloyse Sr helps Danforth Farms become Framingham
  - Howard, *History of Framingham*, 3

- Cloyse to Clayes
  - Clayes is likely the 18th/19th Century standarization of Cloyse not a name change as often purported.
- Success in Framingham becoming a Selectman and Grand Juryman
  - Howard, *History of Framingham*, 138, 139
- Framingham Meeting House, becoming members of Framingham Church
  - Howard, *History of Framingham*, 144-145, 150
- Death of Sarah Cloyse
  - Howard, *History of Framingham*, 507
- Sarai becomes Sarah in the Bible
  - Genesis 17:15
- Remarriage and death of Peter Cloyse
  - Howard, *History of Framingham*, 507, Worcester Co. Probate, vol. 12:352-358
- Alice Bridges in Peter's Will
  - According to Lois Payne Hoover in the *Towne Family Geneology* her ranking in the will is in line with the fact that she was not his

natural child. But he still looked after her and cared for her as if she was his own daughter.
- Probate of Peter's Will
  - Middlesex Co. Probate, vol. 12:355
- Petitions and Exonerations of Abigail Faulkner, Sarah Wardwell, and Elizabeth Proctor
  - Rosenthal, Records of the Salem Witch Hunt, Doc. 876, 877
- Exoneration of Rebecca Nurse, Mary Esty, and others
  - Doc. 931

Below is a list of those who lost their lives due to accusations of Witchcraft in Massachusetts before and during the Salem Witch Trials of 1692

~~~

Victims before 1692

Margaret Jones executed June 16th, 1648

Alice Lake executed c. 1650

Goodwife Kendal executed c. 1650

Mary Parsons died May 1651 in jail

Ann Hibbing executed June 19th, 1656

Goody Glover executed November 16th, 1688

And around eighty-two others were accused before the 1692 Salem Witch Hunt

The Victims of the Salem Witch Hunt

Sarah Osbourne died May 10th, 1692 in jail

Infant child of Sarah Good before June 1692

Bridget Bishop executed June 10th, 1692

Roger Toothaker died June 16th, 1692 in jail

Rebecca Nurse executed July 19th, 1692

Sarah Good executed July 19th, 1692

Susannah Martin executed July 19th, 1692

Sarah Wildes executed July 19th, 1692

Elizabeth Howe executed July 19th, 1692

Martha Carrier executed August 19th, 1692

George Jacobs executed August 19th, 1692

John Proctor executed August 19th, 1692

John Willard executed August 19th, 1692

George Burroughs executed August 19th, 1692

Mary Esty executed September 22nd, 1692

Alice Parker executed September 22nd, 1692

Ann Pudeator executed September 22nd, 1692

Margaret Scott executed September 22nd, 1692

Mary Parker executed September 22nd, 1692

Wilmott Redd executed September 22nd, 1692

Martha Cory executed September 22nd, 1692

Samuel Wardwell executed September 22nd, 1692

Ann Foster died December 3rd, 1692 in jail

Lydia Dustin died March 10th, 1693 in jail

And around one hundred twenty five others accused between March 1st, 1692 and November 5th, 1692.

The Mark of Sarah (Towne) Cloyse,
formerly Bridges